The Fancies,
Chast and Noble

I0592996

The Fancies, Chast and Noble

by **J. Ford**

A critical edition
edited by
Dominick J. Hart

The Renaissance Imagination
Volume 12

Routledge
Taylor & Francis Group

First published in 1985 by Garland Publishing, Inc.

This edition first published in 2018 by Routledge
2 Park Square, Milton Park, Abingdon, Oxon, OX14 4RN
and by Routledge
52 Vanderbilt Avenue, New York, NY 10017, USA

Routledge is an imprint of the Taylor & Francis Group, an informa business

Publisher's Note
The publisher has gone to great lengths to ensure the quality of this reprint but points out that some imperfections in the original copies may be apparent.

Disclaimer
The publisher has made every effort to trace copyright holders and welcomes correspondence from those they have been unable to contact.

A Library of Congress record exists under ISBN:

ISBN 13: 978-0-367-18955-6 (hbk)
ISBN 13: 978-0-367-18958-7 (pbk)
ISBN 13: 978-0-429-19955-4 (ebk)

The Renaissance Imagination
Important Literary and Theatrical Texts
from the Late Middle Ages
through the Seventeenth Century

Stephen Orgel
Editor

THE FANCIES, CHAST AND NOBLE

by J. Ford

A critical edition
edited by
Dominick J. Hart

The Renaissance Imagination
Volume 12

GARLAND PUBLISHING, INC.
NEW YORK & LONDON
1985

Library of Congress Cataloging in Publication Data

Ford, John, 1586–ca. 1640.
The fancies, chast and noble.

(The Renaissance imagination ; v. 12)
Bibliography: p.
I. Hart, Dominick J.   II. Title.   III. Series.
PR2524.F3   1985   822'.3   84-21082
ISBN 0-8240-5452-0 (alk. paper)

Printed on acid-free, 250-year-life paper
Manufactured in the United States of America

For Eileen, Dominick, Bernadette, and Martin

CONTENTS

ACKNOWLEDGMENTS

Many people have assisted me in this project, and to all I am grateful. My teachers, Professors John Kimmey and William Kable, provided the criticism, advice, and encouragement which made this work possible. My friend William Kemp was always ready to lend both advice and assistance. Mrs. Maxine Menefee prepared the typescript with a scrutiny and care which I hope it deserved and for which I can only be grateful. Any errors are mine.

Finally, to my wife Eileen and my children Dominick, Bernadette, and Martin I say—thank you.

CHAPTER ONE

I

John Ford was born in 1586. The date of his birth
and the fact that he was the eldest son of a fairly
wealthy landowner are all we know of his youth until 1601,
when he apparently entered Oxford.[1] His stay there, if he
was there at all, was very brief, as in 1602 he was en-
rolled as a member of the Middle Temple, drawn there,
probably, by an uncle who was a member of high standing.
How long he was there, and whether or not he actually completed his studies for a law degree is unknown. We do
know that in 1610 he was expelled from the Middle Temple
for failure to pay his buttery bill, and that in 1617 he
joined in a protest against the requirement to wear caps
in the dining room of the Temple. The fact that he was
there on these two dates does not imply a continuous
residence, but the conjecture is that he was a fairly
regular member of the Temple and that he probably did obtain his law degree.

Ford's father died in the year 1610 and bequeathed
to Ford ten pounds a year, but to each of Ford's two
younger brothers he bequeathed twenty pounds a year. What
this may reflect upon Ford's character we can only guess.
However, in 1616, Ford received an additional bequest from
his uncle of twenty pounds yearly. This combined with the

ten pounds received from his father would have given Ford
a somewhat meager income, though an amount sufficient to
live.

Any attempt to describe what type of person John Ford
was must rest on a shaky foundation. The only direct allusion to Ford's personality is the following small couplet from The Times Poet, a whimsical book of verse on some
of the public figures of the day.

> Deep in a dump John Ford alone was got,
> With folded arms and melancholy hat.

Some critics have attempted to construe this statement to
indicate that Ford was a reserved, shy and melancholy individual.[2] Such a conclusion, weakened by the meager support the couplet would give to any conclusion, is further
weakened by the fact that the author of the couplet may
not have been referring to Ford himself, but to his work
which, as we shall see, makes wide use of Burton's theory
of melancholy. It would be wise, therefore, in discussing
Ford's personality to disregard this couplet and turn to
the testimony of one who furnishes us with rather slim
but authoritative evidence - Ford himself.

The dedications which precede Ford's plays are re-
markable for their lack of sycophantic tone. At a time
when many of his contemporaries were filling their dedications with hyperbolic praise in attempts to secure patronage, Ford's dedications were unusually honest, direct

and independent. Also unlike most of his contemporaries, Ford did not seem to have a patron. Two of his dedications, Love's Sacrifice and The Lover's Melancholy, are addressed to his very good friend, cousin and namesake, John Ford. Others, like The Fancies, though addressed to persons of rank, are typically independent, and make clear that Ford was not seeking patronage. The dedication to The Fancies reads in part as follows. "Endeavour of being knowne to your Lordship by such meanes, I conceive no Ambition; the extent being bounded by Humility, so neither can the Argument appeare ungracious, nor the Writer, in that, without allowance." From this practice it seems likely that Ford was either an extremely honest and sincere individual, or that he had a fairly substantial source of private income. As much as we may wish to corroborate the former, the latter seems to be the most acceptable conclusion. Ford did come from a financially comfortable family, was probably a lawyer, and did have, from his father and his uncle, a yearly income of thirty pounds. This, combined with statements in a few of his dedications to the effect that his plays were merely the product of his leisure hours, does seem to indicate that Ford did have a private and sufficient source of income, and did not rely on his writing to provide his livelihood.[3]

The date of Ford's death is a mystery. He disappears from almost all records after writing his The Lady's Trial in 1638. Theories have ranged all the way from placing his death in the late 1630's or early 1640's to sometime after the Restoration. The only actual evidence we have is two epigrams dated 1639 and 1641 which seem to indicate that Ford was still alive at those times.[4]

His literary career itself can conveniently be divided into three periods. The first period, during which he wrote prose and poetry, runs from 1606 to 1615. During this period his work reveals a marked interest in love, especially among those of aristocratic birth, and in the cult, or the conventions, which surrounded the aristocracy. Fames Memorial, for example, is a poem in honor of the Earl of Devonshire, the lover and later the husband of Lady Rich. His prose and poetry of this period, however, are of little literary value today, though they do serve to show us the early inclination of Ford's mind toward the theories of love and aristocracy which were to have a profound effect on his later dramatic work. The works of this period are:

Fames Memorial (1606) - a poem

Honor Triumphant (1606) - a prose pamphlet

Christes Bloodie Sweat (1613) - a poem

The Golden Meane (1613) - a prose pamphlet

Sir Thomas Overburyes Ghost (1615) - a prose pamphlet
(now lost)

A Line of Life (1615) - a prose pamphlet

The second period of Ford's career runs from 1621 to
1625. During this period he worked on plays, but only in
collaboration with older and more well-known dramatists.
Ford's collaborative efforts include:

The Witch of Edmonton (1621) - Ford, Dekker, and
Rowley

The Spanish Gypsy (1622-3) - Ford, Middleton, and
Rowley

A Late Murther of the Sun Upon the Mother (1624) -
Ford, Dekker, Webster, and Rowley (now lost)

The Bristowe Merchant (1624) - Ford and Dekker (now
lost)[5]

The Faire Maid of the Inne (1625) - Ford and Fletcher

It appears that in most of his collaboration Ford worked
chiefly with single scenes or characters. The detailed
and sometimes delicate work of creating and developing
the plot was more often than not left to a more experienced collaborator.[6] It is without much doubt that this
is one of the major causes of the careless or skimpy plots
which some critics hold often mars his own best dramatic
work.[7]

The third period of Ford's career, during which he produced his own dramatic work unaided, runs from 1628 to 1638. We do not have a date for his last play The Queen, but it was probably written soon after The Lady's Trial. All his plays were produced by either the Queen's or the King's Men at either the Phoenix, the Blackfriars, or the Cockpit. As an examination of his plays reveals, and as he himself tells us in his dedications, all of Ford's plays were directed at the higher class of audience, that is, at the educated, middle, and aristocratic classes, the type of audience which may have formed a regular clientele for the indoor theaters of the period.[8] When compared to his predecessors, Ford's work usually contains a minimum of comic buffoonery designed to please the tastes of the lower classes. This is fortunate since when Ford does employ such buffoonery, it is often inept, indicating either a lack of ability or a lack of concern on the part of the artist, or its comic potential takes second place to a primary function of reinforcing, albeit weakly, the main plot. An exception to this tendency, however, is 'Tis Pity. Here all the subplots are integrated with and necessary to the main plot. They are used to present Annabella's suitors as foils for Giovanni. Also, though Ford's plays were produced by adult companies at both public and private theaters, there was, during Ford's career, a considerable narrowing of the gap that had previously existed between public and private theaters. Thus it is not strange that Ford directed his plays, often performed on the public stage, to the higher classes. The audience of the public theater, was, during the 1630's, fairly well sprinkled with individuals who formerly could be found only at the private theaters.[9]

The following is a list of Ford's own dramatic works. The years assigned to The Broken Heart, Love's Sacrifice, and 'Tis Pity She's a Whore are conjectural. All three of these plays were published in 1633, but it is unlikely that Ford wrote them all in one year. The Fancies, though published in 1638, must have been written before May 12, 1636, the date on which the Queen's Majesties Servants ceased to play at the Phoenix.[10]

The Lover's Melancholy (1628)

The Broken Heart (1631-2)

Love's Sacrifice and 'Tis Pity She's a Whore (1632-3)

Perkin Warbeck (1633-4)

The Fancies: Chast and Noble (1635-6)

The Lady's Trial (1637-8)

The Queen (?)

II

Every age has its own particular prejudices. As the
neoclassicists favored Jonson, so the romanticists favored Shakespeare. Even so, the Victorians, unable to
accept Ford's themes, could not delve beyond them into a
full appreciation of his work. These critics were ap-
palled by the themes of adultery, incest, and illicit
love which crowd Ford's work. Apparently they did not
look beyond the themes. Affronted by the subject matter
of his plays, they almost immediately condemned Ford.
They did not seem to seek either for any legitimate reasons as to why Ford chose such themes, or for any dramatic
value which the themes may have had. They combined this
fault with his loose plots and his occasional use of
sensationalism, two weaknesses which Ford was guilty of,
and dismissed him as, at best, a second-rate dramatist.
This is somewhat ironic as Ford indicates in his dedications that his plays are intended for a thoughtful
audience - an intention recognized and seconded in Edward Greenfield's commendatory poem which precedes The
Fancies.

> These Fancies chast and noble, are no straines
> Drop't from the itch of over-heated braines.
> They speake unblushing truth,
> The guard of Beauty, and the care of youth;
> Well relish't, might repayre
> An Academy, for the young, and faire.
> (To Master John Ford 7-12)[11]

Similarly, in Ford's own prologue to The Broken Heart there
is the following.

> The title lends no expectation here
> Of apish laughter, or of some lame jeer
> At place or persons; no pretended clause
> Of jests fit for a brothel courts applause
> From vulgar admiration: such low songs,
> Tuned to unchaste ears, suit not modest
> tongues.
>
> (Prologue 3-8)[12]

Thus, if those who charge Ford with "decadence" are correct,
either Ford was not as honest as he seems to have been and
the lines from The Broken Heart were a deliberate attempt
to mislead the audience, or such critics failed to evaluate
Ford properly and ignored the warning he himself gives in
these lines.[13] The latter case seems to be the most likely.

More recently, however, readers have sought for and
found some possible reasons as to why Ford chose the themes
that he did and what inducements of his period led him to
his choice. Thus they have been able to comprehend more
fully what Ford's intentions were and have come to a better
understanding of his work, and through this understanding
to a greater appreciation. They have also discovered that
Ford is particularly a product of his age.[14]

Ford was heir to a dual Jacobean dramatic tradition.
On the one hand there was the drama of the Fletcherian
type with emphasis on beautiful light lyric verse, melodramatic situations and sudden and surprise reversals of

fortune. On the other hand there was the drama of the
type characteristic of Middleton, which was more psychological than melodramatic, and whose verse was not as
lyrical as it was realistic.[15] Ford's drama, for the most
part, took the direction of Middleton's.[16] He was often
melodramatic, but in his better moments melodrama was
incidental to his psychological analysis of character.
This is fortunate as Ford's genius was in analysis and
inquiry, not in incident. During this time, however,
dramatists were becoming increasingly aware of the value
of their work as literature. The psychological studies
of Stendhal, Flaubert and Joyce had not yet been written,
and literature to the Jacobeans, at least fiction, necessarily implied a tight plot structure.[17] This view may
have been partly the cause of Ford's attempt to fuse the
earlier form of action drama with his own psychological
drama. One of the results of this attempted fusion is
Ford's adoption of the sometimes unfortunate technique of
many of his contemporaries, that of the spectacular scene.
Examples of this technique are only too numerous in his
work: the Chair device used to trap Spadone in The Fancies, and Ithocles in The Broken Heart; Giovanni carrying Annabella's heart on his dagger in the last scene of
'Tis Pity; and Fernando rising from the tomb in Love's
Sacrifice. Lamentable as these scenes may be, the most

regrettable effects of this attempted fusion were that
it prevented Ford from fully developing his genius and
that it did contribute (though when compared to many of
his contemporaries it was a very small contribution) to
the decay of the unified play into the contrived scene.

Ford's genius for psychological inquiry makes it important to examine the view which Ford had of man and
which he exploited in his drama. The early years of the
seventeenth century saw the emergence of a new science in
which man attempted to find the physical laws of his behavior. Ford could not help but be aware of this new
movement and, more than being just aware, he incorpo-
rated many of its principles into his dramatic work. The
version of the new science with which he was most familiar
and which most influenced his work is that contained in
Robert Burton's The Anatomy of Melancholy. It is true
that this was a popularized version of the new science
of Ford's day filled with many precepts which did not accurately reflect the views of Burton's more academic peers.[18]
Nevertheless, Burton's intention was the same as that of
his peers, that is, to explain man's behavior in physical
terms.[19]

In its early years the new science had concerned itself with man's ethical as well as his physical behavior,
but by the seventeenth century, especially through the

influence of the immensely popular Burton, it had evolved
into an amoral guide devoted almost exclusively to physical behavior. According to Burton man is controlled by
his humours which, in turn, are themselves completely controlled by any object which a man covets. This object may
be either good or bad. Since man is so controlled, he has
no free will and is, therefore, completely dominated by the
object which he covets. It is essential to man's well-
being that he obtain the object which he desires, for if
he does not, his humour involved will burn and produce a
substance called adust. This adust is a poison to man's
system, and its continued presence will yield sickness and
eventual death.[20] Burton's work concerns itself with all
of man's humours and with all of their effects upon man;
but Ford's work betrays a primary interest in the humour
which controls passionate love, and with the effects which
passionate love has upon man.[21]

In Burton there are two categories of passionate
love - heroical love and jealousy. Heroical love is the
passion which precedes marriage; jealousy is the passion
which follows marriage. Though interested in both, Ford
was primarily interested in heroical love. Burton's explanation of heroical love essentially follows his concept
which covers his whole theory of the humours. The individual who desires to possess another man or woman

must attain his goal if he is to prevent his humour from burning and producing the deadly adust. The control which this passion would have over him is such that he would not rest until he obtains the object of his desires, or unless, through some extraordinary means, the object of his desires is somewhat changed. The pursuit which he would undertake would not stop at reasonable means, but, if necessary, would turn to the irrational. This irrational behavior is one of the consequences of adust. Assuming that the individual's passion can not be again subjugated to his reason through diversion to another more accessible object, or through the power of prayer and grace, there is only one possible cure, and that is the possession of the one he desires.[22] There is only one socially acceptable way in which he may possess this individual - marriage, according to Burton "... the last and best refuge and cure of Heroical love...."[23] Marriage, however, may, when impediments exist, be a threat to the established moral order.[24] In fact, this threat of disorder is one of the traits which distinguish heroical love from a normal and natural love free of any impediments.[25] In such a case the victim must either accept the consequences of sickness and death, or indulge in a socially illicit relationship. In view of the dire consequences which would follow the frustration of a passion, Burton questions the social conventions which would prevent a cure.[26]

However far-fetched this theory may sound to the modern mind, much credence apparently was given to it by Burton's contemporaries. In view of Ford's wide use of this theory there is little room to doubt his acceptance of it. However, his acceptance of Burton's scientific theory does not imply that he shared Burton's skeptical view of the value of the socially imposed moral standards of the day. Ford makes no moral judgement in his work. He merely portrays the dilemma into which this widely accepted theory might eventually place man. For this Ford can not be condemned.[27]

The dilemma, of course, does not always occur. There is sometimes the possibility of a cure for the passion, and when a cure does take place, as in Ford's The Lover's Melancholy, the result is a comedy or, at least, a tragicomedy. In this play there are no insurmountable barriers to the unions of the three pairs of lovers. Eroclea is brought back to the pining Duke; Thamasta is eventually reconciled to her lover Menaphon; and Cleophila, once released from the necessity to care for her father Meleander, is free to marry Amethus.

When the dilemma does occur, when there is no possibility of a cure, as in 'Tis Pity She's a Whore and The Broken Heart, the result is tragedy. In 'Tis Pity

Giovanni can not cure his passion for Annabella through marriage as they are brother and sister. Neither is he cured through the Burtonian advice of the friar who first recommends prayer and submission to moral principles, and who, as a last resort, suggests that Giovanni cool his lust with a woman of the streets rather than with his sister. The two, therefore, take the only course open to them and become involved in an illicit and incestuous relationship. This temporarily cures Giovanni's passion until Annabella is discovered to be pregnant. In order to avoid any suspicion arising from her condition, Annabella marries the notorious Soranzo. A marriage arranged, in part, by the friar as a means of ending the affair between Giovanni and Annabella. Presumably it will divert Annabella's passion from her brother to her new husband. This tactic is, however, thwarted by her nurse Putana who discloses Annabella's illicit relationship with Giovanni to Annabella's husband, Soranzo. Their relationship revealed, and Giovanni unable to further indulge his passion, he becomes a victim of the poisonous adust and eventually kills both himself and Annabella. Likewise, in The Broken Heart, Orgilus, unable to relieve his passion for Penthea because of her marriage to Bassanes, murders Ithocles, the brother who arranged Penthea's marriage and comes to grief himself. Also, Calantha, deprived of her love by Ithocles' murder,

dies of a broken heart. It is significant in this play
that we have a third pair of lovers, Prophilus and
Euphranea. These two are not prevented from curing their
passion through marriage, and thus avert the tragic deaths
which befell the others.

Though primarily interested in heroical love, Ford
was also concerned with jealousy. Ford's treatment of
Burton's description of jealousy finds a good example in
The Fancies' Romanello who, thinking himself deceived and
betrayed by his love Castamela, laments.

> I will converse with beasts; there is in
>   mankinde
> No sound society, but in woman (blesse me)
> Nor faith nor reason: I may justly wonder
> What trust was in my Mother.
>   (IV. ii, 1-4)

This clearly seems to echo Burton who says that the jealous
man suspects "...not strangers only, but Brothers and Sisters, Father and Mother, nearest and dearest friends."[28]
Also, Bassanes in The Broken Heart, an old man and therefore very susceptible to jealousy, is so affected by his
jealousy for Penthea that he goes to the ridiculous and
irrational extreme of boarding up the windows of his house
lest through them a passion should develop between Penthea
and another.[29] Fortunately for Bassanes he is cured of
his jealousy through Penthea's death, and of his sorrow for
her death through the duties assigned him by Calantha, a
cure for sorrow very similar to that prescribed in Burton.[30]

Again, in The Lover's Melancholy, we find the physician Corax prescribing Burtonian cures to ease Meleander's sorrow for his missing daughter Eroclea, and Palador's passion of heroical love. Corax's prescription for Palador involves an abandonment of ease, pleasure and courtly life, the principal inducements, according to Burton, of heroical love; and the performance of exercise and other activities designed to divert the Prince's mind from his passions - one of the possible cures suggested by Burton.[31] Likewise, in The Fancies, Flavia's marriage to Julio took place because

> 'Twas thought
> By his Physitians, that she was a creature,
> Agreed best with the cure of the disease,
> His present new infirmity then labour'd in.
> (I. i, 49-52)

Though it is never made explicit what the "infirmity" was, the marriage was probably a cure, the best one according to Burton, for Julio's love melancholy.[32]

III

Thus far we have noted that Ford's drama was highly
psychological in the Burtonian vein, and that it was addressed primarily to the educated and aristocratic classes.
However, another influence at work in Ford's drama, also
strongly connected with its link to the aristocracy, was
a Platonic code of love brought from France by Queen Henrietta Maria. Though the Queen's intentions were to raise
the morals and values of the English Court, there is some
disagreement over her final accomplishment.[33]

The code which Queen Henrietta introduced was a system of courtly etiquette which had been popularized in
France through the influence of the salon of the Marquise
de Rambouillet and by the success of Honoré D'Urfé's Astrèe,
a pastoral romance whose nymphs and shepherds live in a
world of elaborate compliment and debate.[34] The Platonism
which it introduced, however, was not new and earlier examples of it can be found "... in sonnets of Petrarch, the
sixteenth century Italian pastorals, Spanish romance, French
Renaissance poetry and prose, in fact, in such literature
as also inspired the Elizabethan sonnet sequences and pastoral romances."[35] The difference between D'Urfé's use of
Platonism and the others is that D'Urfé molded it into a
complete social system which made its adoption by leisure
laden members of the court easy and appealing.[36] It probably

appealed to them much as an interesting and new diversion, a game. It was very likely not taken seriously in its more austere aspects; rather it "... was Platonism given a gallant or courtly twist; welcomed, as it had been in Italy long before, as an excuse for more zealous love-making, while the extreme 'Platonic' of the poet's imagination, once embodied in the flesh, would have been considered as much a fanatic as the Puritan and not unlike him."[37]

When the Queen arrived in England in 1625 she did not immediately try to impose French manners on the English court. But gradually she began a program to refine the rough English court much as Catherine de Vivonne had refined the French court earlier in the century.[38] Thus in 1633, with the Queen herself taking a part, Walter Montague's The Shepherd's Paradise was performed at court, a play in which the "... rules of Platonic discipline are illustrated with painful fullness of detail."[39] From this point on preciosite was to be a popular, if controversial, subject at court.[40]

As summarized by G. F. Sensabaugh, the precepts of love and etiquette which Queen Henrietta Maria introduced are: that fate rules all lovers, therefore lovers have no choice; that beauty and goodness are one and the same; that beautiful women are souls to be worshiped, and, therefore, to be the principal objects of men's desires;

that true love is of equal hearts and divine, that is,
true love is of the soul not the body; and finally that
love is all important and all powerful, therefore it is
more important and more powerful than reason.[41] It is
readily discernible how this theory could complement and
enhance Burton's theory of melancholy. The concept that
fate rules all lovers is much akin to Burton's theory of
the absence of free will which occurs when a man becomes
dominated by the object he covets. The concept that love
is all important and all powerful and, therefore, above
reason can easily be allied with Burton's theory of the
irrational behavior produced by adust. That Ford had this
theory of love in mind, as well as Burton's theory of humours, seems probable, especially when we note such scenes
as the following in the second act of 'Tis Pity. Giovanni
is attempting to convince the Friar of Annabella's virtue
by a description of her physical beauty.

> It is a principle which you have taught,
> When I was yet your scholar, that the frame
> And composition of the mind doth follow
> The frame and composition of [the] body:
> So, where the body's furniture is beauty,
> The mind's must needs be virtue; which allow'd,
> Virtue itself is reason but refin'd,
> And love the quintessence of that: this proves,
> My sister's beauty being rarely fair
> Is rarely virtuous; chiefly in her love,
> And chiefly in that love, her love to me:
> If hers to me, then so is mine to her;
> Since in like causes are effects alike.
>   (II. v)[42]

This would be an interesting bit of pseudo-logic if
Giovanni were not seriously trying to justify an incestuous relationship with his sister.   Such perversions of
the Platonic code, in which love, or passion, takes precedence over all moral and social bounds, coupled with his
usual themes of adultery and incest have caused some
critics to conclude that Ford approved of the activities
which his themes treat.   For example, one critic concluded
his attack on 'Tis Pity with the following.

> So far from acting as a stern censor of such
> criminal aberrations as occur in this play,
> Ford looks upon them with a lenient sym-
> pathetic eye.   Passion and sin, even when of
> so revolting a nature as in the present in-
> stance, are represented as irresistible, so,
> that it is useless to fight them.   Besides,
> they are surrounded by a lot of argument
> which may cause the merely objective spec-
> tator to distrust his own notions of good and
> evil, and to palliate the ugliness of what
> is morally indefensible.   This is very objec-
> tionable, for just as it goes against the
> grain to see crime and vice made subjects
> for laughter it should rouse our indignation
> to see pity and sympathy involved for that
> which really only deserves our scorn and
> contempt.[43]

There has, however, been a re-examination of Ford's pre-
sumed approval of the activities which his themes treat. Most
modern critics conclude that Ford was not bringing characters into conflict with the moral order simply to create
effective theatre, but to show the tragic results of depen-
dence on passion rather than reason.   Invariably these critics point out that in Ford's tragedies all the heroes

and heroines who allow their passions to gain sway over
their reason are killed. Giovanni, they say, loses a
full understanding of his guilt. This wins our sympathy,
but it brings about his own tragic death in a manner re-
miniscent of Macbeth. Fernando and Biancha in Love's
Sacrifice are less guilty, but no less unfortunate. They
have enough control over their passions to prevent them
from consummating their love, but not enough to prevent
their tragic death. Likewise, Perkin is punished for his
unjust rebellion against the rightful king. Turning from
Ford's tragedies to his tragicomedies, these critics point
out that in the tragicomedies there is no real moral reason
why the characters, such as the lovers in The Lover's Melancholy, should suffer; therefore they do not. But con-
fining our attention for the moment to the tragedies, we
must disagree. The one crucial point which these critics
either ignore or fail to properly credit is that we sympathize with all these characters who meet their deaths.[44]
We sympathize with them just as we sympathize with a Lear,
a Hamlet, or an Othello. But unlike Lear, Hamlet, or
Othello there is no victory in their deaths, no final understanding of why they have suffered and must die, of what
the value of their suffering and death is, or of what their
role has been in an ordered universe. They suffer, die,
and that is the end. Ford is a poor dramatist if he sends

these characters to their deaths merely for convenience's
sake, merely to punish evil properly. He would be guilty
of a gross incongruity, obtaining and holding our sympathy
for his characters and then, without changing our attitudes
or feelings, punishing them as evil. But Ford is not a
poor dramatist.

Una Ellis-Fermor is more nearly correct when she suggests that Ford does away with the problem of evil by convincing us that evil never existed.[45] She says that in
Ford's drama sin is not overthrown but converted. Such a
theory can easily be reconciled with and can draw some
very convincing proof from an appeal to the concepts of
individualism and Platonic love current in Ford's day.
But this theory would have to maintain that Ford accepted
the corrupted version of the Platonic code, that Ford
thought an individual's attainment of the object of his
passion through any means outside the conventional moral
code was just. To say that Ford felt that evil never
existed and that he converted, not overthrew, sin is
merely another way of saying that Ford reversed the traditional moral code. This is the primary reason for which
Ford has been condemned as decadent, and if it is true,
the charge is not without validity.

But we feel the theory is not true. We would alter
Miss Ellis-Fermor's theory and say that Ford did not do

away with the problem of evil by convincing us that it
never existed, did not convert rather than overthrow sin,
but created a group of characters who did. There is an
enormous difference between saying that his characters did,
rather than Ford. This is why his characters die without
losing our sympathy and without coming to a final realization of the reasons for their fate. Ford's characters are
victims, not of passion but of reason. Their passion has
not overcome their reason, but their reason has become
permanently distorted.[46] In the first scene of 'Tis Pity
we see Giovanni not giving utterance to a passion for
Annabella, but calmly, though falsely, explaining to the
Friar why his and Annabella's very kinship in blood ap-
proves an incestuous relationship. In Love's Sacrifice
the very friendship of Ferdinand for the Duke becomes a
justifying reason for the adulterous love of Ferdinand and
Biancha; and, sadly, in the last scene we see the Duke himself become subject to this very same distorted reasoning.
Our sympathy is with these characters because they believe they are acting justly.[47] But unlike Hamlet, Lear,
or Othello there is no final victory or understanding for
these characters because the reason, the right reason which
holds sway in the last scenes of Shakespeare's tragedies,
no longer exists in Ford's. Reason has not been overcome,
unable to rise again triumphant at the end. It has been

distorted, and in the distortion it has been destroyed. Perhaps this is the key to the mystery of <u>Perkin Warbeck</u>. Perhaps Ford sees Perkin as not pretending to be the rightful heir to the throne, but actually believing that he is so. This may be why Perkin goes to his death without renouncing his claim. He would not renounce what he thought truly his.

In the combination of Burton's theory of humours and the corrupted code of Platonic love, Ford seemed to see an indissoluble dilemma. In the first man could lose his free will; in the other man corrupted his reason. It is one thing for Giovanni to commit incest with his sister, for Ferdinand to have an adulterous affair with his friend's wife, and for Perkin to desire a throne that is not his; but quite another for these characters to find their passions right, just, and reasonable. Ford has been called both an immoral and an amoral writer. Certainly he is not immoral, but perhaps he is not amoral either. If under Burton's theory man can not control his passions, certainly he can control his reason. But if man's reason is corrupted or distorted as it could be under the Platonic love code, then man's passion, if it is going to lead to his death, will result in a death with which no one, despite the strictest moral standards, can be unsympathetic. A paranoiac killer who slays a dozen innocent people may retain our sympathy, though we do not of course sympathize with his actions. So too Ford should not be condemned because of the sympathy he gives to his licentious characters. To Ford they are as innocent of intentional evil as is our killer.

Ford's tragedy is not the tragedy of the Greeks or of Shakespeare. It is a tragedy of pathos, a tragedy without hope. This lack of hope may also partly explain why the endings of his tragicomedies always seem to be unsatisfactory. The characters in both the comedies and tragedies are, as indicated earlier, the same. Only the circumstances and, because of the circumstances, the endings differ. There is no growth or change in either, but at least in the tragedies the heroes are forced to carry through with a death that is somehow ennobling. In the tragicomedies, however, the hero is simply bailed out by circumstances. R. J. Kaufmann said that the essence of Ford's tragedy is that the characters do not know themselves. They can not read their own motives, and consequently a situation hardens until it becomes irreducible.[48] Perhaps this is the reason for the death of tragedy in our own day. Perhaps like Ford's characters our reason is distorted and we do not know ourselves. Unlike Shakespeare's characters, we and Ford's characters do not have the reason with which to see into and beyond our situation. Like Ford

we are without hope and can produce only pathos. In this
sense Ford was truly a prophet.

To create this kind of drama it is necessary to foster
within the audience a greater than normal sense of detach-
ment from the play. Without it, the audience would be in
danger of agreeing with and binding itself to, for at least
the moment of the play, the tangled reasoning of a Giovanni, Ferdinand, or Orgilus. This seems to have been a mistake not only of Ford's critics, but of his contemporary
audience as well. It is, however, an error difficult to
avoid within the limits of any single play because of the
apparent innocence of so many of these characters. Further it is one which is responsible for the peculiar power
of Ford's best play, Perkin Warbeck. Nevertheless, it is
not what Ford intended. Perhaps a natural annoyance at
being misunderstood prompted the almost irritated disclaimer of any deliberate bawdiness found in the Prologue,
quoted above, to The Broken Heart. More importantly, for
our own purposes, such an annoyance may be the key to an
understanding of The Fancies.

IV

The _Fancies_ has frequently and perhaps justly been
dismissed as Ford's worst play. Not the least of the
faults often cited is the clumsy and awkwardly contrived
plot structure. Actually there are three plots, joined
by only the barest structural links. Further, within
the plots themselves, each one of which could easily be
presented as a separate entertainment, each new scene de-
pends not so much on what precedes it as it does upon
some new and unexpected twist. Unlike most of Ford, this
play is Fletcherian. Its growth is by accretion rather
than organic; its predominant ingredients are melodrama
and surprise.[49]

The main plot revolves about a deliberate hoax.
Octavio, who is actually benevolent and wise, has for
years successfully convinced all but his closest associates that he is a foolish old lecher who keeps a bower of
Fancies, or young girls, for his private amusement. Apparently to please Octavio, his nephew Troylo convinces
Livio, a would-be gallant and courtier, to contribute his
ward and sister, Castamela, to Octavio's bower. Any com-
punction Livio may have about such a betrayal yields to
Troylo's promise of place and fortune, and his assurances
that Octavio is impotent and can with women do only "...
what his outward sences can delight in" (II. ii. 57). The
court, however, appears to indulge in a corrupt form of

Platonic love. Though this point is not emphasized, it is made fairly evident in Octavio's first advances to Castamela. Here Octavio refers to the lady as a "Soveraigne" whose "yea and nay is law" (III. iii. 194). He also indulges in the following bit of Platonic reasoning.

> Oct.   Love deare Maid,
> Is but desire of beauty, and 'tis proper
> For beauty to desire to be belov'd.
>
> (III. iii. 203-205)

Castamela is, of course, angered by her brother's betrayal and refuses to have anything to do with Octavio until he assures her that his intentions are in no way dishonorable, and until she learns from the Fancies that, far from being Octavio's concubines, they are his nieces whom he has both shielded from the world and schooled in every grace. The deceit, it is explained, was employed to test the depth of affection between Castamela and her suitor Romanello, and to draw Castamela and Troylo closer together. The plan works. Romanello's love is found wanting, and Castamela and Troylo are betrothed. Fortunately for Livio, he tries to undo his betrayal before the truth is revealed in the last scene. For this rather tardy act of virtue, he is rewarded by Octavio with the hand of one of the Fancies.

A secondary plot concerns Romanello, his sister Flavia, Flavia's former husband Fabricio, and her present

husband Lord Julio. Fabricio, a bankrupt merchant, was
very much loved by Flavia, but to redeem himself financially he sold Flavia to Julio. The exchange was accomplished by the legal ruse of claiming that before Flavia
and Fabricio were married, there existed a "... precontract unto another" (II. i. 110), presumably a betrothal.
The subsequent marriage between Flavia and Fabricio was
thus rendered null and void.[50] Presumably because of
Flavia's practicality and good grace, the marriage between herself and Lord Julio is successful. Flavia does,
however, have some regrets. First, for some incom-
prehensible reason, she still loves Fabricio and grieves
at his continued misfortune. She intercedes on his be-
half with her present lord, and is relieved to discover
in the last scene of the play that Fabricio has mended
his ways and has become a Capuchin monk. Second, Flavia
regrets the estrangement that exists between her brother,
Romanello, and herself. As protection against the advances of two of Lord Julio's retainers, Flavia has assumed "A port of humorous anticknesse in carriage" (IV.
ii. 43). She was too kind-hearted to report the advances
to Julio for fear it would cost the retainers their lives.
Romanello, unaware of her motives and already offended
by her second marriage, thinks she is taking her position
too lightly and disowns her. However, in the fourth

act a confrontation between Flavia and her brother reunites
them.

The comic subplot is a rather bawdy piece typical of
Ford. In it the foul-mouthed old crone Morosa, who is
also a guardian to the Fancies, is married to Secco,
Octavio's young barber. Before the wedding festivities
are over though, Spadone, a supposed eunuch, gulls Secco
into thinking that he has been cuckolded by Troylo's servant, Nitido. There is much slapstick humor and many
jokes about impotence and cuckolds before Secco learns the
truth and takes his revenge on Spadone. As the play ends
Morosa and Secco are reconciled, Spadone is revealed as no
eunuch and a friend of the court; and Morosa is exonerated
as a somewhat scatological but good old dame who has done
well by the Fancies.

With the exception of Flavia there is nothing subtle
about either the plot construction or character development. A crucial stimulus in the play, Livio's reformation
from greed to his concern for Castamela's honor, is un-
prepared for and apparently gratuitous.[51] Even the subplot which involves Flavia rests upon the somewhat incredible premise that a woman who has been bought by her
present husband from her former husband can now capture
the love of both and the reformation of the former. Finally, in the incredible last scene there is Troylo's sudden

declaration of love for Castamela, Romanello's convenient
realization that he doesn't love Castamela, and the awkward
announcement that Fabricio, the man who sold his wife, has
gone and turned Capuchin. This is all in addition to the
deceit perpetrated as to the true nature of both the Fancies and their guardian, Morosa.

It is not surprising, however, that what subtlety and
psychological insight there is in this play principally
involves Flavia. Ford's Elizabethan predecessors had focused their attention on the minds of great men. Ford
focused his on the mind of the ordinary man. Though his
characters may have the title of Duke or Lord, they are
lacking those ennobling qualities of mind and spirit which
constitute greatness. In The Fancies all the characters
in the main plot, with the exception of Flavia and Romanello, are nominally aristocratic, yet none but Flavia are
truly noble. Each is something of an opportunist, and all
engage in some form of selfish deceit. Thus in The Fancies
it is only with Flavia that there is an example of what
T. S. Eliot calls Ford's true art. It is found, says
Eliot, in the "slow solemn rhythm" which was "Ford's dis-
tinct contribution to the blank verse of the period."[52]
It is also found in character which is revealed not
through sententious or grandly eloquent speeches but
through "... the brief mysterious words, so calm in

seeming, which well up from the depths of despair. He concentrates the revelation of a soul's agony into a sob or sigh. The surface seems calm: we scarcely suspect that there is anything beneath...."[53] One such instance occurs in the third act after Flavia has coldly dismissed Fabricio from her presence. As she turns to Julio, however, she can no longer completely control her grief, but does manage to conceal it in a scene of quiet anguish.

> Fla.   Prithee sweetest,
> Harke in your eare. ---- Beshrew't, the brim of
>   your hat
> Strucke in mine eye. --[Aside] Dissemble honest
>   teares
> The griefes my heart does labour in ----smarts
> Unmeasurably.
>
> Jul.   A chance, a chance, 'twill off,
> Suddenly off. Forbeare, this handkercher
> But makes it worse.
>
> Cam.   Wincke madam with that eye.
> The paine will quickly pass.
>
> Ves.   Immediately,
> I know it by experience.
>
> Fla.   Yes, I finde it.
>   (III. ii. 97-105)

Such passages are, though, rare in The Fancies, and

the play has more often been singled out for its crudity.
Some measure of how the play has been regarded can be
gauged from the Harper's Family Library edition which
bowdlerized the "unfit" parts and produced a remnant of
500 lines. But in light of such reaction it seems odd
that in the dedicatory poem to John Ford printed with the
play, the author, Edward Greenfield, should both sneer at
the "wits of th' Universitie, or Court" and recommend the
play as "An Academy for the young, and faire."

An explanation of this seemingly incongruous situation has recently been offered by Juliet Sutton in her
article "Platonic Love in Ford's The Fancies, Chaste and
Noble."[54] Miss Sutton points out that both the main plot
and the subplots are based on false suspicion, that the
notion of misunderstanding so pervades the play as to become its theme, and is, in fact, the reason why throughout
the play there is a constant play on the word "fancy,"
which has the meaning of both an amorous inclination and
a groundless supposition. Misunderstanding extends to the
audience as well, but only, according to Miss Sutton, because the audience is inclined to think the worst. For
example, in the initial interview between Troylo and Livio,
Troylo never actually says that Octavio's Fancies constitute a seraglio; it is left to Livio to think the worst,
and the audience naturally agrees with Livio. Again,

in the second interview between these two, Troylo describes
the Fancies.

> Such as are gentle-born, not meanely; such
> To whom both gawdinesse and apelike fashions
> Are monstrous; such as cleanlinesse and decency,
> Prompt to a vertuous envy; such as study
> A knowledge of no danger, but themselves.
>   (II. ii. 78-82)

This, however, has no effect on the attitudes of either
Livio or the audience. It is, Miss Sutton claims, as if
neither were listening. Other examples are the interviews
Castamela has with first Morosa and then Octavio. In the
first she is scandalized by her own suspicions, and in the
second she ignores everything that Morosa has said and
everything that Octavio is saying, and accuses Octavio of
advances which he has not made. Yet the audience tends to
agree with Castamela. Finally and ironically it is Castamela who, herself suspected of corruption by Romanello,
utters the charge that is at the heart of the play and
that applies in part to its audience as well as its
characters.

> Cas.   Romanello, know
> You have forgot the noblenesse of truth
> And fixt on scandall now.
>   (I. iii. 36-38)

All have "fixt on scandall" - Livio, Castamela, Romanello,
Camillo, Vespuci, Secco, and the audience. This may well
be what Ford intended and what he was referring to in his

Prologue where he writes

> His free invention runnes but in conceit
> Of meere imaginations; there's the hight
> Of what he writes, which if traduc'd by some
> 'Tis well (he sayes) he's farre enough from home.
> For you, for him, for us, then this remaines:
> Fancie, your own opinions, for our paines.
> (Prologue 11-16)

In other words it is up to Ford's audience to imagine
what they will of the characters and situations in the
play; and if they choose to imagine the worst, it is their
own and not his doing. Considered thus, Ford deliberately
sets out to entrap his audience as well as his characters.
Whether or not the trap is contrived and unfair is arguable.
Miss Sutton claims it is not, that it is simply a matter of
Ford knowing what his audience would be most likely to
"fancy" when given the choice he presents to them. In
fact, however, the audience, if not the characters, is
given little choice. The play opens in the middle of a
conversation between Troylo and Livio. It is immediately
clear that Troylo has proposed something extraordinary con-
cerning Castamela to Livio, though exactly what is not
stated. Nevertheless, the whole tenor of the conversation
["'Tis but a goodly pandarisme" (I. i. 55); I must resolve/
To turne my sister whore" (I. i. 125-126)] leaves little
room for any conclusion other than the one all audiences
inevitably reach. Nor are there any clarifying solilo-
quies or asides, devices which could easily have been

utilized to enlighten an audience.[55] Finally, any con-
firmation an audience may need for its conclusion is provided by the presence of Morosa, a dame who seems eminently qualified to be mistress to a quartet of whores.

Contrived or not, the play is in many ways a joke on
its audience, and one which Ford's Prologue seems to indicate was both recognized and deliberate. As such The
Fancies conveys an attitude, if only accidentally, not unlike that of much of modern drama. In fact, there is a
strong temptation to carry the comparison further and suggest that The Fancies has something of the Theater of the
Absurd about it. The continuing cycle of deception and
self-deception, the posturing and the antic, even farcical,
behavior are all there. Troylo deceives Livio, Livio deceives Castamela, and Castamela deceives Livio. Nitido
tricks Romanello into the guise of the misogynist Prugnioli; Spadone gulls Secco into falsely proclaiming himself a cuckold. More importantly, at least two of the
characters are self-deceived.

Romanello believes he is in love with Castamela.
His behavior, however, is rather strange. In the first
scene between the two, Castamela's firm but gentle rejec-
tion elicits from Romanello a violent fit of invective.

> Rom.   A Dogge, a Parrot,
> A Monkey, a Caroach, a guarded lackey,

> A Waiting woman with her lips seald up,
>
> Are pretty toyes to please my Mistresse wanton.
>
> (I. iii. 38-41)

Strange behavior for a suitor, but not for one afflicted
with love-melancholy and one of its effects - jealousy,
which according to Burton can drive a man to carelessly
charge his love with being "... a strumpet, a light-house-
wife, a bitch, an arrant whore."[56] Romanello's condition
is obvious and is recognized even by Nitido, the page who
arranged for Romanello's entry into Octavio's court disguised as Prugnioli. After making the arrangements, and
gulling Romanello out of his purse into the bargain,
Nitido exclaims "... Love, oh love,/ What a pure madnesse
are thou?" (III. i. 80-81). Even the disguise itself,
assumed principally to spy on Castamela, is typical of the
jealous man who, like Bassanes in The Broken Heart, goes
to such extremes that he will hunt "... after every word
he hears, every whisper, and amplifies it to himself (as
all melancholy men do in other matters) with a most unjust calumny of others, he misinterprets every thing is
said or done, most apt to mistake or misconster, he pries
into every corner, follows close, observes to an hair."[57]
Romanello's melancholy and jealousy, however, is in one
way unlike that described by Burton. It is not grounded
in any real affection Romanello might feel for Castamela.

In fact Romanello's affections themselves are, he is told
by Octavio, founded on "... meerely Courtship" (V. iii.
99). By "Courtship" Octavio apparently means that Romanello's interest "... had been less in Castamela than in expressing his own melancholy."[58] Thus Romanello's melancholy has been the product of self-deception. He had assumed the role of rejected suitor just as he had assumed
the role of Prugnioli, and had succeeded, in both cases,
at fooling no one but himself. Like other of Ford's
characters Romanello's melancholy and jealousy are real,
but they are irrational, the product of a disordered mind.
Romanello, however, is fortunate enough to be cured by
being brought face to face with the foolishness of his own
antic behavior when the true nature of the Fancies is revealed and by his own admission of "Frenzy, how didst thou
seize me!" (V. iii. 121)

Livio is the other self-deceived character. Unlike
Romanello he is a victim of ambition. But by succumbing
to Troylo's casuistry and resolving to turn his sister
whore, Livio succeeds only in being rebuffed by his own
conscience. He strives unsuccessfully to affect the po-
lite decadence which he seems to believe is appropriate and
customary in courtly circles. Thus almost as soon as he
commits himself to Troylo and accepts Octavio's preferment, he begins to have regrets. Not, though before he

makes a fool of himself by strutting like a peacock,
as much in costume as Romanello was when disguised as
Prugnioli.

> Liv.   Sister, look yee,
>   How by a new creation of my Taylors,
>   I've shooke off old mortality. The rags
>   Of home spun Gentry (prethee sister marke it)
>   Are cast by, and I now appeare in fashion
>   Unto men, and am receiv'd. Observe me sister--
>   The consequence concernes you.
>   (I. iii. 53-59)

Like Romanello Livio is cured by being made to face his
own foolishness. This is accomplished by Castamela, who
pretends that she enjoys her role as supposed concubine,
by Romanello, who casts Livio's arguments against marriage
back in his teeth (IV. ii. 145-150), and by the revelation that Castamela, like the Fancies, is still unsullied.
Just as Livio's cure is similar to Romanello's so is his
reaction which takes the form of an admission of his own
lack of insight. Castamela, he says, has been "Much more
worthy/ A better Brother, he [Troylo] a better Friend/ Then
my dull braines could fashion" (V. iii. 94-96).

Livio and Romanello are not, however, the only characters in The Fancies who play roles. Octavio, Flavia,
and, in the subplot, Spadone and Morosa, all appear at one

time or another to be what they are not. The difference
is that these latter consciously assume their various roles
and do so with a clear purpose in mind. To protect the
Fancies and to enhance Troylo's prospects with Castamela,
Octavio pretends to be a lecher; to both cure her brother
and teach him a lesson, Castamela pretends to enjoy a role
as concubine; to protect herself from the advances of
Camillo and Vespuci, and to hide her sorrow and disappoint-
ment from Julio, Flavia assumes an "anticknesse in carriage." The utter lack of self-deception in their roles
throws into relief the positions of Livio and Romanello.
It also represents a very practical compromise in their
positions between a complete honesty and frankness which
could be devastating to both themselves and others, and
complete deception. Theirs is the "white lie." This practical approach extends in some cases to their view of love
and marriage. Romanello yields all to what he thinks is
affection; Livio yields all to advancement. Flavia and
Castamela, however, manage to combine sentiment with practical considerations. Thus Flavia is able to adjust to her
marriage with Julio, a marriage she could not avoid, to
both their benefits. Likewise, Castamela refuses Romanello
for, among other reasons, the "narrow bands" of both their
fortunes. (See I. iii. 1-25.) Finally, the attitudes of
the Fancies themselves are such that in a spirit of

practical wisdom they can tolerate the prurience of Morosa
and the excesses of Romanello and Livio while retaining
their own propriety. This realistic, rational approach
to problems and situations is both impossible and unaccept-
able to Romanello and Livio before they are cured respectively of jealousy and misconceptions of courtly behavior.
As a result they are cast into ridiculous postures, Romanello as the bombastic Prugnioli, and Livio as the brotherly
pimp turned chastity's watchdog, and they are made the
butt of a great many jokes. Neither do they deceive anyone, and in their roles play only the fool to themselves.[59]

Similarly in the subplot, while Spadone and to some
extent Morosa are purposely playing roles, Secco is un-
wittingly gulled into believing himself a cuckold. So
convinced is he that he insists, despite evidence to the
contrary, on public affirmation of the cuckoldry. Interestingly, Secco swings from the same extremes of adoration
and damnation as does Romanello in his attitude toward
Castamela. When Secco first appears (I. ii), he is mouth-
ing what sounds suspiciously like a bastard form of Platonic love, but before Spadone is finished with him, Secco
is calling his beloved Morosa a "filthy" crone (III. iii.
141-142). The situation is, of course, ridiculous, and
its main intent is humor. The very ridiculousness of
Secco's position, however, does underscore the positions

of Romanello and Livio who like Secco both make public
asses of themselves. Also, Secco's reaction to his own
folly is similar to Romanello's and Livio's. "Enough,"
he says to the teasing Morosa, "I am wise, and will be
merry" (V. ii. 54). The reactions of all three, Romanello,
Livio and Secco, are typical of comedy where "Human dignity
... may get bedaubed; its colors may be hauled down alto-
gether as restraint gives way to incontinence of whatever
kind; but comic personages seldom do more than shake their
heads over the loss."[60]

In fact, though it does have some serious moments,
The Fancies is basically comic, even at times farcical.
This is, it seems, often overlooked by those critics who
bother to comment extensively on the play, and who, as a
whole, tend to take the proceedings rather a bit more
seriously than Ford intended. It is difficult to imagine,
for instance, how the last scene of the play, with all its
revelations, including Vespuci's ludicrously timed news
that Fabricio has become a monk, could be played completely
straight. If not farcical, the scene is at least comic,
and intentionally so.[61] It is no accident that the play
ends in marriage and dancing, a traditional close for
comedy.[62] In The Fancies Ford chose to treat those themes
of love, jealousy, social convention, and ambition with a
considerably lighter touch than in some of his other work.

But like most comedy, especially that which has an element of satire in it, The Fancies is not without its serious purpose. In it the delusions of such characters as Romanello and Livio are stripped away, and they are assisted "... toward the sort of self-knowledge out of which true happiness springs...."[63] It is important, however, not to emphasize the serious purpose too heavily, else there is the risk that the spirit of the play will be misconstrued. Like its closing dance The Fancies is a "harmlesse recreation," which shows

> ... how love oreswayes
> All men of severall conditions; Soldier,
> Gentry, foole, scholler, Merchant man, and
>   Clowne.
>   (V. iii. 129-131)

NOTES TO CHAPTER ONE

[1]A good account of what is known of Ford's life can be found in M. Joan Sargeaunt's John Ford (1935; rpt. New York: Russell, 1966), pp. 1-16.

[2]Havelock Ellis, ed., John Ford, the Mermaid Series (London: Ernest Benn, n.d.), p. viii.

[3]Ford's implications in his dedications that his plays were the products of his leisure hours should not be taken too literally. The amount of work he produced, especially between the years 1631 and 1634, though not comparable to many of his contemporaries, would seem to indicate that much more than a few idle hours were devoted to writing plays.

[4]R. G. Howarth, "John Ford," Notes & Queries, NS 4 (1957), p. 241.

[5]Harold James Oliver, The Problem of John Ford (Carlton, Victoria: Melbourne University Press, 1955), p. 8. I have closely followed Mr. Oliver's dating of the dramatic works.

[6]Oliver, p. 46.

[7]Ellis, p. xiv.

[8]Dorothy M. Farr, John Ford and the Caroline Theater (New York: Barnes and Noble, 1978), p. 7.

[9]Alfred Harbage, Shakespeare and the Rival Traditions (1952; rpt. New York: Barnes and Noble, 1968), pp. 47-57. Also, Alfred Harbage, Cavalier Drama (1936; rpt. New York: Russell, 1964), pp. 149-155.

[10]Gerald Eades Bentley, The Jacobean and Caroline Stage (Oxford: Clarendon Press, 1956), III, p. 443.

[11]All references to The Fancies are keyed to the present edition.

[12]John Ford, The Broken Heart, ed. Brian Morris, The New Mermaids (London: Ernest Benn, 1965), p. 7.

[13]See Stuart P. Sherman, "Ford's Contribution to the Decadence of Drama," John Ford's Dramatische Werke, ed. W. Bang, Materialien zur Kunde des Alteren Englischen Dramas (Louvain: Librairie Universitaire, 1908), XXIII, vii-xix.

[14]For example Ronald Huebert, John Ford: Baroque English Dramatist (Montreal: McGill-Queen's University Press, 1977), places Ford firmly within the baroque tradition of the first half of the seventeenth century.

[15]Marvin T. Herrick, Tragicomedy (1955; rpt. Urbana: University of Illinois Press, 1962), pp. 261-280.

[16]Una Ellis-Fermor, The Jacobean Drama: An Interpretation, 2nd ed., rev. (London: Methuen, 1947), pp. 227-229.

[17]For comparison of Ford to modern writers whose chief interest is psychological inquiry see Ellis' introduction to his John Ford and M. Joan Sargeaunt's John Ford, pp. 123-124.

[18]A similar case can be found today in the somewhat inaccurate view many laymen have of Freud's principles gleaned from the many popular and simplified books on the subject.

[19]G. F. Sensabaugh, The Tragic Muse of John Ford (Stanford: Stanford University Press, 1944), pp. 13-93. Sensabaugh's book was the first to examine in depth Ford's debt to Burton. However, it has since been further studied by Lawrence Babb in his The Elizabethan Malady (1951; rpt. East Lansing: Michigan-State University Press, 1965), and challenged by David L. Frost, The School of Shakespeare (Cambridge: The University Press, 1968), who finds Ford's use of Burton, and Platonism as well, to be very superficial.

[20]Robert Burton, The Anatomy of Melancholy, eds. Floyd Dell and Paul Jordan-Smith (1927; rpt. New York: Todor Publishing Company, 1938), pp. 148-155, (1.1.3). For the convenience of those using other editions, all references to The Anatomy of Melancholy will cite, in addition to page number, partition, section, member and, where applicable, subsection.

[21]Sensabaugh, pp. 24-34.

[22]Mark Stavig, John Ford and the Traditional Moral Order (Madison: University of Wisconsin Press, 1968), pp. 69-71.

[23]Burton, p. 819. (3.2.5.5).

[24]Stavig, p. 72.

[25]Stavig, p. 72 and Burton, pp. 653-656. (3.2.1.2).

[26]Burton, pp. 798-820. (3.2.5.5).

[27]Mark Stavig, op. cit., argues Ford does make an at least implicit judgement in favor of the traditional moral order. However, Stavig has been challenged effectively by S. Gorley Putt in "The Modernity of John Ford," English 18 (1969), 47-52 and Harriet Hawkins in "The Morality of Elizabethan Drama: Some Footnotes to Plato," English Renaissance Studies Presented to Dame Helen Gardner in Honor of her Seventieth Birthday, ed. John Carey (Oxford: Clarendon Press, 1980), pp. 12-32. Both Putt and Hawkins essentially argue for the artistic ethical neutrality of the dramatist. Finally, Ronald Huebert, op. cit., pp.192-201, argues that Ford is more properly labelled "baroque" rather than "decadent," and that with this recognition should come the realization that ethical choice was not Ford's principal concern or dramatic focus, but that exploration of man's "emotional nature" was.

[28]Burton, p. 841. (3.3.2).

[29]Babb, p. 141.

[30]Burton, pp. 532-540. (2.3.5).

[31]Burton, pp. 765-770. (3.2.5.1).

[32]Burton, pp. 798-820. (3.2.5.5).

[33]G. F. Sensabaugh (The Tragic Muse of John Ford) feels that Platonic love was so corrupted by the English courtiers as to present a challenge to the sanctity and even advisability of marriage. On the other hand, Alfred Harbage (Cavalier Drama, p. 36) maintains that for the most part the Platonic code provided a harmless diversion for the court. Mark Stavig's recent study (John Ford and the Traditional Moral Order) suggests that the practice of the code at court remained basically innocent, but that its arguments were susceptible to perversion (Stavig,

p. 40). In Stavig's view the perversion of "... justi-
fiable Platonic admiration of beauty and virtue ..." into
"... diseased, heroical love ..." furnishes one of the main
themes in Ford's work (Stavig, p. 191). See Alfred Horatio
Upham, The French Influence in English Literature (1908;
rpt. New York: Octagon Books, 1965), pp. 334-339 for a
brief review of some contemporary literary comments on the
problems of a perverted Platonism.

[34]Kathleen M. Lynch, The Social Mode of Restoration
Comedy (1926; rpt. New York: Octagon Books, 1965),
pp. 43-44.

[35]Lynch, p. 45.

[36]Lynch, p. 46.

[37]Upham, p. 331.

[38]Upham, p. 309.

[39]Lynch, p. 57.

[40]Harbage, Cavalier Drama, p. 36.

[41]Sensabaugh, The Tragic Muse, pp. 109-119.

[42]John Ford, "'Tis Pity She's A Whore," The Works of
John Ford, eds. William Gifford and Alexander Dyce (1895;
rpt. New York: Russell, 1965), I, 146.

[43]J. A. Bastiaenen, Elizabethan Literature (London,
1887), from H. J. Oliver, The Problem of John Ford,
pp. 4-5.

[44]See, for example, Clifford Leech, John Ford and
the Drama of His Time (London: Chatto & Windus, 1957).
Also Peter Ure, "Cult and Initiates in Ford's Love's
Sacrifice," MLQ, 11 (September 1950), pp. 298-306. See
also Stavig, op. cit.

[45]Ellis-Fermor, p. 245.

[46]Ronald Huebert, op. cit., pp. 129-136, maintains
the rhetoric of Ford's characters is not the rhetoric of
the Renaissance - an expression of logic, but the baroque
rhetoric of the seventeenth century - a vehicle for emotional and psychological expression and persuasion.

[47] Stavig, p. 191.

[48] R. J. Kaufmann, "Ford's Tragic Perspective," _Texas Studies in Literature and Language_, 1 (Winter 1960), pp. 522-537.

[49] John F. Danby, _Poets on Fortune's Hill_ (1952; rpt. Port Washington, New York: Kennikat Press, 1966), pp. 157-162.

[50] Glenn H. Blayney, "Convention, Plot and Structure in _The Broken Heart_," _MP_, 56 (Aug. 1958), pp. 1-9. Mr. Blayney points out that the custom of betrothal was a common one at the time, and that the vows of betrothal usually took precedence over any subsequent marriage vows. He also convincingly argues that in _The Broken Heart_, contrary to the view that Ford was reversing the traditional moral order by presenting the love of Orgilus and Penthea as having precedence over the marriage vows of Penthea and Bassanes, Ford was actually writing a problem play dealing with the then current problem of forced marriages.

[51] See Stavig, p. 81 for an opposite view of Livio's change of heart.

[52] T. S. Eliot, _Selected Essays: 1917-1932_ (London: Faber and Faber, 1932), p. 195. See also Huebert, _op. cit._, pp. 208-209, who takes issue with the general notion that Ford's best poetic style is restrained.

[53] Ellis, pp. xiv.

[54] _Studies in English Literature_, 7 (Spring 1967), 299-309.

[55] Dorothy M. Farr, _op. cit._, pp. 155-156, points out that Ford seldom makes use of soliloquy or clarifying speeches of any sort, that Ford's plays are thus very malleable in performance, subject to varied interpretation by actor, director, and audience. This situation supports the case made for the importance of the accidentals to Ford's text as argued in Chapter Two of this book.

[56] Burton, p. 842. (3.3.2).

[57] Burton, p. 840. (3.3.2).

[58] Stavig, p. 82.

50

[59]Cyrus Hoy, The Hyacinth Room (New York: Alfred A. Knopf, 1964), p. 191.

[60]Hoy, p. 200.

[61]See Huebert, op. cit., pp. 123-124, for a different reading of the effect of the final scenes of The Fancies.

[62]Hoy, p. 17.

[63]Hoy, p. 113.

CHAPTER TWO

The Fancies, Chast and Noble, was first published in
1638. This single quarto edition provided the only copies
of the play until 1811, when Henry Weber edited The Dramatic
Works of John Ford. Since Weber, six, or possibly seven,
more editions have appeared.[1] Of these only four have any
textual significance. The remaining three consist of a
text bowdlerized beyond recognition, an unacknowledged reprint of an earlier edition, and an edition which probably
never existed. The first of these three is the interesting,
but puritanical, Harper's Family Library edition published
in 1831, with a joint New York and London imprint. In
this edition a play of well over two thousand lines was
somehow reduced to approximately six hundred lines. The
editors' greatest achievement is the fifth act. They reduced it to fifteen lines. The reason for the pruning was,
of course, the rather indelicate language of the subplot,
and the liberal use of double-entendre throughout the play.
Next, we have Hartley Coleridge's edition of The Dramatic
Works of Massinger and Ford. This was first published in
1840 and apparently proved popular as it was reissued four
times - in 1848, 1851, 1864, and 1875. The text of Coleridge's edition, however, is simply a reprint of that
edited by William Gifford and published in his The Dramatic

Works of John Ford in 1827. Finally, there is the possible
edition of the play in the supposed three volume set The
Works of John Ford, edited by A. H. Bullen and published in
1895. The only evidence for the existence of this edition,
though, is a bibliographical entry in Samuel Tannenbaum's
bibliography of Ford in his series Elizabethan Bibliographies.[2] Tannenbaum lists it as a possible revision of
Gifford's 1827 edition. He acknowledges never having seen
a copy, but does not explain on what he bases his conjecture that it is such a revision. Since no other record of
this edition can be found, the probability is that it
never existed. Also, there is a possible explanation of
Tannenbaum's error. An edition of The Works of John Ford
was published in 1895. The editors were William Gifford
and Alexander Dyce, but the publishers were Lawrence and
Bullen of London. Tannenbaum lists this edition, but perhaps he recorded it twice - once correctly, and once er-
roneously listing Bullen as the editor. Interestingly
enough, there is no publishing information, other than
the date, given in Tannenbaum for the edition supposedly
edited by Bullen.

Of the four other editions which succeeded Weber we
have already alluded to two - William Gifford's 1827 The
Dramatic Works of John Ford and The Works of John Ford
edited by both Gifford and Alexander Dyce. This last was

originally published in 1869, but a new edition with "additions" was published in 1895. Although a copy of the 1869 edition has not been available for examination, Peter Ure in his Methuen edition of Perkin Warbeck notes that these "additions" consist only "of a prefatory 'Note' by A. H. B[ullen] in the first volume and a reprint of Henry Goodcole's pamphlet about Elizabeth Sawyer the witch."[3] This last edition was reproduced and reissued by Russell & Russell, Inc. in 1965. Finally, there is also the edition found in Henry De Vocht's Materials for the Study of Old English Drama, Louvain, 1927.

All of these editions rely in varying degrees upon the 1638 quarto. Weber, of course, being the first of the modern editors, had no other source but the quarto for his text. Weber's text has been collated for the apparatus of this edition and, as should be expected, there are a number of substantive variants between it and the quarto. The greatest area of discrepancy between the two texts, however, involves what are hesitantly called the accidentals - punctuation, italics, and capitalization. Weber completely modernizes the punctuation and arbitrarily deletes and adds both italics and capitals. Such changes might be of little significance to the text of another author's play, but Ford seems to employ these devices both more extensively and more purposefully than most. It is a habit with

Ford, seen in other plays besides The Fancies, to use
italics and capitals for emphasis. Ford's punctuation is
in need of some emendation for the modern reader. Particularly it is in need of periods to indicate full stops -
something Ford rarely supplies. However, the bulk of his
punctuation, though frequently unusual, does seem to consciously suggest the desired emphasis and inflection. Other changes which Weber made were to provide scene divisions, add to and enlarge upon the quarto's functional but
sparse stage directions, and to indicate which lines he
felt were spoken as asides or were not meant to be heard
by all the characters on the stage. This is something
which the quarto either indicates with dashes or does not
indicate at all.

William Gifford's 1827 edition followed Weber's and
relied heavily upon it. This reliance is seen most immediately in the arrangement and format of the preliminary
matter, the scene divisions, and the stage directions. In
each of these matters Gifford consistently follows Weber
wherever Weber differs from the quarto. Gifford's reliance upon Weber also includes the use of Weber's notes.
Gifford did, however, have access to a copy of one of the
1638 quartos for in a number of instances he restored an
original reading altered by Weber. As with Weber, though,
there are a number of substantive variants between

Gifford's text and the quarto. Also, Gifford, even more
so than Weber, arbitrarily revises Ford's careful use of
punctuation, italics and capitalization. Gifford's text
has been collated for the apparatus of this edition.

Also collated was the 1965 reproduction of the 1895
text edited by Gifford and Alexander Dyce. This edition
together with the 1869 one was Dyce's revision of Gifford's 1827 text. Dyce's contribution consists of both
adding his own and enlarging upon Gifford's notes, and of
the restoration of a number of correct readings from the
quarto which had been lost since the time of Weber's edition. The Gifford-Dyce text does, on the whole, seem to
be better and more carefully edited than any of the other
nineteenth century texts. There are, however, the usual
number of substantive variants, and the same criticism in
regard to the accidentals as was applied to the previous
editions can be applied also to this one.

The last edition published appeared in 1927, in Henry
de Vocht's continuation of Bang's Materialien series. An
apparently accurate reproduction of an unidentified copy of
the quarto formerly in the possession of Wilhelm Bang, De
Vocht's predecessor, this edition is, unfortunately, without any editorial apparatus.

Since no edition after the original 1638 quarto pos-
sesses fresh textual authority, I have decided to use the

quarto as the basis for this text. The copy chosen, British Museum number 644. b. 39, has been collated with the following additional copies: Chapin, Bodleian (1), Folger, Huntington, Harvard, and Yale Elizabethan Club. These collations revealed a minimum of variants between the quartos. In fact there are only four substantive variants. These occur on pages B3^V, C3^V, K1^V, and K2, and are recorded in the appendix. As there is not an unusual number of typographical errors and apparent misreadings, the quarto was probably both composed and proofread rather carefully. Such care would be in keeping with the consistent work habits which the following study indicates were followed by this shop.

The quarto was printed with the following title page:

THE/FANCIES,/Chast and Noble://PRESENTED BY THE/ Queenes Maiesties Servants,/At the Phoenix in/ Drury-lane.//Fide Honor.//LONDON,/Printed by E. P. for Henry Seile, and are to be sold/at his shop, at the Tygers Head in Fleetstreet,/over-against Saint Dunstans/Church. 1638.

"Fide Honor" is John Ford's familiar anagram. E. P. was Elizabeth Purslowe, the widow of George Purslowe. Their shop, both before and after George's death, undertook the printing of a number of dramatic quartos, many of them, as was The Fancies, for Henry Seile. As might be expected from an experienced shop, The Fancies is rather carefully printed. There is, for example, little evidence of jamming even though, as later evidence will indicate, the first half of the play was probably set by forme and thus had to be cast off.

The collation of the quarto is $A^4(A1+a^2)B-K^4$. The title page is on A1, with $A1^V$ being a blank page. The text begins on A2 and runs through K4; $K4^V$ is also a blank page. The half sheet a, which was probably produced after the rest of the play, contains "The Epistle Dedicatorie," a1 and $a1^V$; a commendatory poem "To John Ford," a2; and the author's "Prologue," $a2^V$. Also, contrary to the usual practice, although not without parallels, the pages of the quarto, beginning with the first page of the text, are numbered. However, the most striking physical character- istic of the quarto is its clear division into two parts, with the break coming at the exact middle of the text, be- tween signatures E and F. The most conclusive evidence for this break comes from spelling tests and a running title analysis.

The running title for the entire play is simply The Fancies; however, it offers enough evidence to establish

firmly the existence of a break in the printing of the
text and to suggest strongly the order in which the sheets
were composed and printed. Thus an analysis of the type
used in the running title indicates the presence of four
skeleton formes. These formes, though, are not alternated
throughout the text, but are paired, with only one pair
being used in each half of the play. Skeleton formes I and
II are used through signature E; skeleton formes III and IV
are used for signatures F through K. The first and most
obvious indication of the existence of the two pairs of
formes is a perceptible change in the type size of many of
the letters of the running title, beginning with F1. This
change is most apparent with the letters "$\underline{T}$" and "$\underline{i}$."
Starting with F1 the "$\underline{T}$" is visibly smaller on almost every
page of the second half of the play than its counterpart
in the first half. It does not occur only on pages F3 and
G3. Similarly "$\underline{i}$" occurs on more than half the pages of
the second part. It does not occur on pages F2, F4, F4^V,
G2, G4, G4^V, H1, H2, H2^V, H4, I1, I2, I2^V, I4, K1, K1^V,
K2, and K3.

Other substantial evidence consists of spacing and
damaged type, and is set forth in the chart to be found in
the appendix. What the evidence shows, however, is that
the first half of the play was set with two skeleton formes
used in the following manner:

Skeleton Forme I	Skeleton Forme II
Outer A	Inner A
Inner B	Outer B
Outer C	Inner C
Inner D	Outer D
Outer E	
Inner E	

It is possible that since both the outer and inner formes of
signature E were imposed in the same skeleton, the pages of
this signature were composed by forme rather than seriatim.
More substantial proof, however, is the recurrence in the
text of a damaged 's' on $D2^V$ and D2, and a damaged 'L' on D3
and $D3^V$. If signature D were set seriatim, distribution of
type would had to have occurred between D2 and $D2^V$, and
then again between D3 and $D3^V$. This is highly unlikely;
thus it is very probable that signature D, at least, was
set by forme. No such strong evidence exists for the other
signatures in the first half of the text, but it may be
conjectured that if one or two signatures were set by forme,
the others may also have been. Further, the regular alternation between inner and outer formes also suggests, if
only faintly, composition by forme. If the signatures were
set seriatim, the tendency would probably be for one skeleton to be used with all the outer signatures and one with
the inner. Such a tendency would be especially true of a
shop that worked as regularly and systematically as Purslowe's seems to have done; and, in fact, this is exactly
the situation we find in the second half of the play,

signatures F through K, which was in all probability set seriatim.

Thus the two skeleton formes of the second half of the play were used in the following manner:

Skeleton Forme III	Skeleton Forme IV
Inner F	Outer F
Inner G	Outer G
Inner H	Outer H
Inner I	Outer I
Outer K	Inner K

Now these formes could as easily have been set by forme as seriatim were it not for the switch evident with signature K. Why should the skeleton which had been regularly used for the outer formes of signatures F through I suddenly be used for the inner forme of signature K? And vice-versa? The answer would seem to be that in seriatim composition the inner forme is finished first. Therefore it is the first into and the first out of the press, and the same skeleton is consequently used for the inner forme of the next signature. This is the situation in our text for signatures F through I. However, in signature K, $K4^V$ is a blank page. As a result, and unlike signatures F through I, outer K (K1, $K2^V$, and K3) would be completed before inner K. Hence we find outer K imposed in the skeleton forme used for the inner formes of F through I. Seriatim composition is also attested to by the lack of any evidence of

jamming which casting off would have made probable, especially in the prose portions of the play. It should be
noted that this last is an argument which at first seems
to work against the probability of the first half being
composed by forme since there too there is little evidence
of jamming. However, page 6, line 6 and page 8, lines 12
and 25 are possible instances of jamming. Moreover the
compositor of the first half of the play seems to have used
the stage directions rather than the lines of the play to
space out his pages. Thus, while the spacing for the stage
directions is consistent (with one exception) in the second
half of the play, this same spacing is regularly inconsis-
tent in the first half of the play.

It is naturally impossible to know what caused the
break in the text and why, but there is enough evidence for
some interesting speculation as to what might have happened.
We know, for instance, that two new skeleton formes were
used in the second half of the play. We also know that one
of the skeletons used in the first half of the play was
dropped at what seems to be a rather inconvenient time,
that is, before any of signature E was completed. A reason
for this may be that another job which had to be done immediately was in the wings, but could not be started until
a chase was made available. Although the skeleton could
have been left standing outside the chase, a chase may have

been provided at the earliest moment by disassembling skeleton forme II after outer D had been printed off. Skeleton forme I was kept intact for the imposition of signature E, which may have been composed before the new job arrived.[4] When E was completed, this skeleton forme may also have been disassembled to make available another chase. The significance of such a situation would be to indicate a scarcity of available chases and to provide an example of a play text being interrupted in the middle of its printing. Evidence that such was the situation, or, at least, that the break was a real and prolonged interruption, and not just the result of an accidental breaking of the skeleton forme, is seen in the change of method of composition between the two halves of the text from by forme to seriatim. Seriatim composition strongly suggests that at any one time there is just one compositor for the second half of the play as two would tend to get in each other's way. Composition by forme, on the other hand, does little to resolve the question of the number of compositors at work, though the suspicion would be that there were two. Neither spelling tests nor a study of the speech prefixes have completely resolved this issue. However both do indicate that the compositor of the second half of the play did not compose the first half. If nothing else, such a situation would further support the thesis that the break in the text was a substantial one.

For the sake of convenience a chart of all the spelling tests which were made will be found in the appendix.
There will also be found there a list of the variant forms
of speech prefixes. The most significant spelling tests
involved variant forms of the pronoun for the second person
singular and plural, and the third person singular. There
are three variants of the second person pronoun found in
the text - 'ye,' 'yee,' and 'you.' There are four variants
of the third person pronoun - 'he,' 'hee,' 'a',' and 'a.'
The form 'yee' is found with uniform frequency through the
complete text of the play. The form 'you' is also found
in both halves of the play, but it occurs only twice in the
first half, on $D3^V$ and $E2^V$, while it occurs rather frequently in the second half of the text. The form 'ye,' however,
is not found until F1, the first page of the second half,
and then it occurs as frequently as 'yee.' A similar situation arises in the use of the third person singular pronoun. The form 'hee' is used infrequently in both halves,
and is found chiefly with contractions and in cases of
special emphasis. The form 'he,' like 'yee,' is found
equally throughout the play. The form 'a',' however, occurs only in the first half of the text, and the form 'a'
occurs only in the second half. A pattern is clear. Both
the forms 'ye' and 'a' are completely eschewed in the first

half of the play, but are used regularly in the second half. The reverse is true of 'a'.' Further, there seems to be a much greater inclination toward the use of 'you' in the second than in the first half of the text. Such variants indicate that the same compositor did not set both halves of the play. These variants are also noteworthy in that they corroborate the existence of a break in the text between signatures E and F. Other words which tend to substantiate this pattern, but which occur too infrequently to establish it are 'go' and 'goe,' and 'em' and ''em.' Also the tendency to drop the apostrophe, which the second compositor reveals in his use of the contraction 'a,' is sometimes carried over into the past participle. Thus, while the first compositor regularly uses an apostrophe when the 'e' of the ending 'ed' is omitted, the second compositor will frequently use simply 'd.' Examples can be found at $G4^V$line 29, H2 line 33, $H3^V$ line 25, F4 line 12, and G4 line 10.

An analysis of the speech prefixes neither corroborates nor disputes the pattern established by the running-title analysis and spelling tests. It does, though, present some evidence of a further pattern in the second half of the text. Thus the speech prefix 'Li.' for Livio is used exclusively through signatures F and G. After that it does not occur. Instead the prefix 'Liv.' is used

exclusively through signatures H, I, and K. This corre-
sponds to a pattern discerned in the use of 'ye' and 'yee'
in the second half of the play. With one exception (Gl)
'ye' is used exclusively through signatures F and G. But
through signatures H, I, and K 'ye' and 'yee' are used with
uniform regularity. Finally, in the second half of the
text, the contraction 'a' is, with one exception (Hl), used
only in signatures F and G. (It is interesting to note
that this exception occurs in a prose portion of the play,
the same circumstances in which the single use of this contraction in the first half of the play occurred.)[5] Consequently there is room for speculation that two compositors
worked on the second half of the play, one composing signatures F and G, another, signatures H, I, and K. Two compositors working in this manner would not conflict with the
hypothesis of seriatim composition as only one man would
be composing at a time. In fact, the concurrence of such
a pattern with seriatim composition tends to confirm both.
One other admittedly tentative bit of evidence can be added.
The running title chart shows that all the pages produced
in skeleton forme III and the pages through signature G
produced in skeleton forme IV correspond, that is, the
parallel pages of each gathering have the same running
title. This correspondence does not extend, however, to
the pages of signatures H and I produced in skeleton forme

IV. The reason for this lack of correspondence is that beginning with signature H skeleton forme IV was turned around. Thus H1 has the same running title as G3, H2^V as G4^V, H3 as G1, and H4^V as G2^V. This change may be coincidental, but combined with the evidence of the spelling tests, it does suggest that somewhere between signatures G and H the normal routine was interrupted. This disturbance could very well have been caused by the arrival of a new compositor.

An attempt to establish the stages in the process of composition at which distribution of type took place has met with only limited success. There is, however, enough evidence to establish, at least within wide margins, when several distributions occurred. The evidence consists solely of damaged type. An effort to use as evidence the substitution of individual pieces of type for ligatures, and vice-versa, proved inconclusive. The evidence that there is points to a minimum of at least three distributions in the first half of the text. The first distribution is identified by the recurrence of a damaged 'b' on C2^V and D1, a damaged 'A' on C4^V and D1, and a damaged 'N' on B2 and D3. Since the first half of the text was probably set by forme, the most logical point for this distribution would be between the composition of inner and outer C. The second identifiable distribution almost certainly took place between outer and inner D. Such is likely since the four damaged types which serve as evidence recur in outer and inner D. They are the damaged 'A' on D1 and D4, the damaged 'b' on D1 and D3^V, the damaged 'S' on D2^V and D2, and the damaged 'L' on D3 and D3^V. A third distribution is indicated by the recurrence of a damaged 'A' on D4 and E3^V, and a damaged 'w' on D4 and E4. Since a distribution had already occurred between outer and inner D, it seems unlikely that this distribution would have taken place before one forme of signature E was composed. Finally since the existing evidence points to distribution between the inner and outer formes of C, D, and E, it would not be baseless to postulate that either one or two previous distributions took place between the inner and outer formes of both signatures A and B.

The evidence for distribution in the second half of the play is less conclusive than that for the first, but it does indicate that there were at least three distributions. The evidence is the recurrence of a damaged 'O' on F4^V amd H3^V, a damaged 'f' on H3 and I1^V, a damaged 'D' and 'b' on I2^V and K4, a small 's' on H3^V and I1^V, and a damaged 'E' on H3 and K3. Together, the damaged 'O' and 'E' would seem to pinpoint a distribution between H3 and H3^V. But the small 's' indicates a distribution between H3^{V}and I1^V. It is unlikely that two distributions occurred within such close proximity. Thus the first distribution probably took place well before H3. Finally, a third distribution somewhere between $I2^V$ and K4 is indicated by the damaged 'D' and 'b'. Though any attempt to place more accurately these distributions must, on such evidence as is available, be a guess, I feel it is quite probable that the type was distributed between $F4^V$ and G1, $H4^V$ and I1, and $I4^V$ and K1. Also, I feel that another distribution, for which there is no overt evidence other than the regular habits of the compositor, took place between $G4^V$ and H1. If the conclusions on distributions are correct, it means that the type was distributed every eight pages or after each signature.

The most important conclusion to be drawn from this study, indeed from the entire analysis of the printing of the play, is the mundane but significant fact that the printers worked carefully and followed faithfully a set pattern. It would be hoped that such a careful shop would adhere closely to the text of whatever they were printing. Textual fidelity is important with Ford, for as noted at the beginning of this chapter, the accidentals (punctuation, italics, and capitals) play a relatively significant role in his texts. Of course, if the print-shop is to reproduce accurately what Ford wrote, it must use good copy. The copy used for The Fancies seems to have been good; at

least it does not appear to have been foul-papers as the
speeches are all correctly assigned, entrances and exits
are carefully marked, and there is generally none of the
confusion one would expect to find in a quarto based on
foul-papers. In fact, the quarto seems to have been based
on a prompter's copy which may have been reproduced from
some other manuscript, possibly the author's fair copy, or
it may have been the fair copy edited to serve as a prompt
book. Evidence for this is found principally in the stage
directions. These directions are extremely sparse, but are
extremely careful to note the movements of the actors and
any elaborate stage business. Also, there is one page
(E1) on which a stage direction has been entered in the
margin, not the usual place. Possibly it was squeezed in
by the compositor. But it is also possible that the direction was placed in the margin of the printer's copy by the
prompter. On the other hand there are no written voice
directions, such as "aside" - an element which would be of
little concern to a prompter, or necessary to an actor.
Further, as the chart of speech prefixes indicates, there
is a noticeable tendency for the characters' names to be
written out in full when they first appear in the play.
After that there generally occur a number of abbreviations
for each name until a final form is settled upon. This
does not necessarily point to a prompter, but it does seem

to indicate the hand of a copyist. It is much more probable for a copyist to be unaware of the proper abbrevi-
ation for a character's name than it is for the author.
Thus my own speculation as to the nature of the printer's
copy is that it was a text prepared specifically for the
play-house, and was probably copied by a professional
scribe from the author's fair copy.

In preparing the text an attempt was made to retain
the punctuation of the quarto wherever possible, as the
punctuation often seems to be a reflection of Ford's own
habits. However, since the quarto uses colons, semicolons,
and dashes for changes of direction and rhetorical flour-
ishes where modern English can only limply use commas, fidelity to the quarto has frequently been impossible. One
characteristic that has been retained, though, is the use
of parentheses for both asides and the vocative case. In
any event, virtually all instances where this text does not
follow the quarto have been recorded in the textual notes.
The only exceptions are the speech prefixes which have been
regularized, the substitution of the modern 'J' and 'U'
where the quarto sometimes uses 'I' and 'V' and those stage
directions where the only difference between the two texts
is the quarto's use of italics. Other typographical fea-
tures such as the old long 's,' and an occasional use of
small capitals have been silently emended. Also, though

the quarto does not often provide specific voice directions, such as, asides, they have been included in this text where clarity demands it. They have not been recorded in the textual notes, but are always placed in brackets. Finally, the scene divisions followed here were first supplied by Weber. There is, however, no question as to where they occur.

NOTES TO CHAPTER TWO

[1] For a complete compilation of all editions following the quarto see the list on Page 73.

[2] Samuel Tannenbaum, John Ford: A Concise Bibliography, Elizabethan Bibliographies, No. 20 (New York, 1941), p. 10.

[3] Peter Ure, ed., The Chronicle History of Perkin Warbeck: A Strange Truth, The Revels Plays (London, 1968), p. xxvii.

[4] It is possible, but very unlikely, that both halves of the play were produced simultaneously on two presses.

[5] For a study of the influence of justification on compositorial spelling habits see William S. Kable, "The Influence of Justification on Spelling in Jaggard's Compositor B," Studies in Bibliography, 20 (1967), 235-239.

PREVIOUS EDITIONS AND REPRINTS OF THE FANCIES

Ford, John. The Fancies, Chast and Noble. London:
Henry Seile, 1638.

_____. The Dramatic Works of John Ford. Ed.
H. Weber. 2 vols. London: Longman, Hurst, Rees,
Orme, Brown, Miller, and Murray, 1811. Vol. II.

_____. The Dramatic Works of John Ford. Ed.
W. Gifford. 2 vols. London: John Murray, 1827.
Vol. II.

_____. The Dramatic Works of John Ford. Harper's
Family Library Dramatic Series, No. 4. New York:
J. & J. Harper, 1831.

_____. The Dramatic Works of John Ford. The
Family Library Dramatic Series, No. 6. London:
J. Murray, 1831.

_____. The Dramatic Works of Massinger and Ford.
Ed. H. Coleridge. London: E. Moxon, 1840. Reissued in 1848, 1851, 1864, and 1875.

_____. The Works of John Ford. Eds. William
Gifford & Alexander Dyce. 3 vols. London:
J. Toovey, 1869. Vol. II.

_____. The Works of John Ford. Eds. William
Gifford & Alexander Dyce. 3 vols. London:
Lawrence and Bullen, 1895. Vol. II.

_____. John Ford's Dramatic Works. Ed. Henry
De Vocht. Materials for the Study of Old English
Drama, NS. Louvain: Librairie Universitaire,
1927. Vol. I.

_____. John Ford's Dramatic Works. Ed. Henry
De Vocht. Materials for the Study of Old English
Drama, NS. 1927; rpt. Vaduz, Liechtenstein: Kraus
Reprints, Ltd., 1963. Vol. I.

_____. The Works of John Ford. Eds. William
Gifford & Alexander Dyce. 3 vols. 1895; rpt.
New York: Russell & Russell, 1965. Vol. II.

CHAPTER THREE

THE FANCIES, CHAST AND NOBLE

TO THE RIGHT NOBLE Lord, The Lord Randell Mack-

    Donnell, Earle of <u>Antrim</u> in the Kingdome

    of <u>Ireland</u>, Lord Viscount <u>Dunluce</u>.

My Lord,

      Princes, <u>and</u> <u>worthy</u> personages <u>of</u> <u>your</u>

owne eminence, <u>have</u> <u>entertained</u> Poems of this

Nature, <u>with</u> <u>a</u> <u>serious</u> <u>welcome</u>. <u>The</u> Desert <u>of</u>

<u>their</u> <u>Authours</u> <u>might</u> <u>transcend</u> mine, <u>not</u> <u>their</u>

<u>study</u> <u>of</u> service. A <u>practice</u> <u>of</u> <u>Courtship</u> <u>to</u>

Greatnesse, <u>hath</u> <u>not</u> <u>hitherto</u>, <u>in</u> <u>me</u>, <u>aym'd</u> <u>at</u>

<u>any</u> <u>thrift</u>: <u>yet</u> <u>I</u> <u>have</u> <u>ever</u> <u>honored</u> vertue, <u>as</u>   11

<u>the</u> <u>richest</u> <u>ornament</u> <u>to</u> <u>the</u> Noblest Titles.

<u>Endeavour</u> <u>of</u> <u>being</u> <u>knowne</u> <u>to</u> <u>your</u> <u>Lordship</u> <u>by</u>   13

such meanes, <u>I</u> <u>conceive</u> <u>no</u> Ambition; <u>the</u> ex-

tent <u>being</u> <u>bounded</u> <u>by</u> Humility, <u>so</u> <u>neither</u> <u>can</u>   15

<u>the</u> Argument <u>appeare</u> <u>ungracious</u>, <u>nor</u> <u>the</u>   16

Writer, <u>in</u> <u>that</u>, <u>without</u> <u>allowance</u>. <u>You</u> en-

<u>joy</u> (<u>my</u> Lord) <u>the</u> <u>generall</u> <u>suffrage</u>, <u>for</u>

<u>your</u> <u>freedome</u> <u>of</u> merits. <u>May</u> <u>you</u> <u>likewise</u>   19

<u>please</u>, <u>by</u> <u>this</u> particular presentment, <u>amongst</u>

<u>the</u> <u>number</u> <u>of</u> <u>such</u> <u>as</u> <u>faithfully</u> <u>honor</u> those   21

merits, <u>to</u> <u>admit</u> <u>into</u> <u>your</u> Noble <u>construction</u>,

                    John Ford.

To Master John Ford, of the middle Temple, on

    his Bower of Fancies.

I Follow faire Example, not report,

Like wits of th' Universitie, or Court,

    To shew how I can write

At mine owne charges, for the Times delight;

      But to acquit a debt,

Due to right Poets, not the counterfeit.

These Fancies chast and noble, are no straines

Drop't from the itch of over-heated braines.   10

    They speak unblushing truth,

The guard of Beauty, and the care of youth;

      Well relish't, might repayre

An Academy, for the young, and faire.

Such labours (friend) will live; for though some new

Pretenders to the Stage, in hast pursue

    Those Laurels which of old

Enrich't the Actors; yet I can be bold,   18

      To say, Their hopes are sterv'd;

For they but beg, what Pens approv'd deserv'd.

                     Edw. Greenfield.

THE SCENE,

SIENA.

Prologue
                                                  •

The Fancies! that's our Play; in it is showne
Nothing, but what our Author knowes his owne
Without a learned theft. No servant here   3
To some faire Mistris, borrowes for his eare,
His locke, his belt, his sword, the fancied grace
Of any pretty ribon; nor in place
Of charitable friendship, is brought in
A thriving Gamester, that doth chance to win
A lusty summe, while the good hand doth ply him,
And Fancies, this, or that, to him sits by him.
His free invention runnes but in conceit
Of meere imaginations; there's the hight   12
Of what he writes, which if traduc'd by some,
'Tis well (he sayes) he's farre enough from home.
For you, for him, for us, then this remaines: 15
Fancie, your own opinions, for our paines.   16

1   Act I

[I. i]

                Enter Troylo Savelli, and Livio.

        Troy. Doe, doe, be wilfull, desperate, 'tis   1
        manly,
Build on your reputation, such a Fortune
May furnish out your Tables, trim your liveries,
Enrich your heirs, with purchase of a Patrimony
Which shall hold out beyond the waste of riot,
Sticke Honours on your Heraldry, with titles
As swelling and as numerous, as may likely
Grow to a pretty volume. Here's eternity.   8
All this can reputation, marry can it,
Indeed what not?

        Liv. Such language from a Gentleman
So noble in his quality as you are
Deserves in my weake Judgement rather pittie
Then a contempt.

        Troy. Could'st thou consider Livio
The fashion of the times, their study, practice,
Nay, their ambitions, thou would'st soone dis-
        tinguish
Betwixt the abject lownesse of a poverty,

And the applauded triumph of abundance,

2   Though compast by the meanest service. Wherein   18

Shall you betray your guilt to common censure,

Waiving the private charge of your opinion

By rising up to greatnesse, or at least

To plenty which now buyes it?

    Liv.   Troylo-Savelli,   22

Playes merrily on my wants.

    Troy.   Troylo-Savelli   23

Speakes to the friend he loves, to his owne Livio.   24

Looke prethee through the great Dukes Court in

    Florence,

Number his favorites, and then examine

By what steps some chiefe Officers in state

Have reach't the height they stand in.

    Liv.   By their merits.   28

    Troy. Right, by their merits. Well he

    merited   29

Th' Intendments o're the Gallies at Ligorne,

Made grand collector of the customes there,

Who led the Prince unto his Wives chaste bed,

And stood himselfe by, in his night gowne, fear-

    ing

The theft might be discovered: was't not handsome?   34

The Lady knowes not yet on't.

Liv.   Most impossible.   35

Troy.   He merited well to weare a roabe of

Chamlet,

Who train'd his Brothers daughter (scarce a girle)

Into the Armes of Mont-Angentorato,

Whiles the young Lord of Telamon, her husband,   39

Was packetted to France, to study courtship,

Under forsooth a colour of employment.   41

Employment, yea of honour.

Liv.   Y'are well read   42

In misteries of state.

Troy.   Here in Sienna,   43

Bold Julio de Varana Lord of Camerine,   44

Held it no blemish to his blood and greatnesse,

From a plaine Merchant with a thousand Ducats

To buy his wife, nay justifie the purchase.   47

3 Procur'd it by a dispensation from Rome,   48

Allowed and warranted. 'Twas thought   49

By his Physitians, that she was a creature,

Agreed best with the cure of the disease,

His present new infirmity then labour'd in.

Yet these are things in prospect of the world,

Advanc'd imploi'd, and eminent.

Liv.   At best   54

'Tis but a goodly pandarisme.

    <u>Troy</u>.   Shrew businesse.

Thou child in thrift, thou foole of honesty!   56

I'st a disparagement for gentlemen,

For friends of lower ranck, to doe the offices   58

Of necessary kindnesse without fee   59

For one another - courtesies of course,   60

Mirthes of society - when petty mushroomes,   61

Transplanted from their dunghils spread on

    mountaines,

And passe for Cedars by their servile flatteries

On great mens vices? -- Pander -- th'art deceived.   64

The word includes preferment. Tis a title   65

Of dignity. I could adde somewhat more else.   66

    <u>Liv</u>. Adde any thing of reason

    <u>Troy</u>.   Castamela!   67

Thy beautious sister like a precious Tissue,

Not shapt into a garment fit for wearing,

Wants the adornments of the Workemans cunning

To set the richnesse of the piece at view,

Though in her selfe all wonder. Come Ile tell thee,

A way there may be (know I love thee <u>Livio</u>)   73

To fix this Jewell in a Ring of gold,

Yet lodge it in a Cabanet of Ivory,

White pure unspotted Ivorie. Put case-   76

<u>Livio</u> himselfe shall keepe the key on't?

    Liv.   Oh Sir,

Create me what you please of yours. Doe this,   78

You are another Nature.

4   Enter Octavio, and Nitido.   02

    Troy. Be then pliable   79

To my first rules of your advancement. ---- See,   80

Octavio my good Uncle, the great Marquesse

Of our Siena comes as we could wish-   82

In private. ---- Noble Sir!

    Oct.   My bosomes Secretary,   83

My dearest, best lov'd Nephew.

    Troy. [Aside]   We have beene thirsty

In our pursuit. ---- Sir here's a gentleman   85

Desertfull of your knowledge, and as covetous

Of entertainment from it. You shall honour   87

Your judgment, to intrust him to your favours.   88

His merits will commend it.

    Oct.   Gladly welcome.

Your own worth is a herald to proclaim it.   90

For tast of your preferment, we admit you

The chiefe provisor of our Horse.

    Liv.   Your bounty

Stiles me your ever servant.

    <u>Troy</u>. [Aside]   Hee's our owne,

Surely, nay most perswadedly. ---- My thanks Sir   94

Owes to this just engagement.

    <u>Oct</u>.   Slacke no time

To enter on your fortunes. --[Aside] Thou art

    carefull   96

My <u>Troylo</u> in the study of a duty.   97

His name is <u>Livio</u>!

    <u>Liv</u>.   <u>Livio</u> my good Lord.

    <u>Oct</u>. Again y'are welcome to us. [Aside]

    Be as speedy   99

Deare Nephew as th'art constant. ---- Men of parts,   100

Fit parts and sound are rarelie to be met with,

But being met with, therefore to be cherish'd,

With love and with supportance. While I stand,   103

<u>Livio</u> can no way fall. ----

                Yet once more welcome.   104

                  Exit Octavio and Nitido.   03

    <u>Troy</u>. An honourable liberality,

5 Timely dispos'd without delay or question,

Commands a gratitude. Is not this better   107

Then waiting three or foure months at livory,

With cup and knee unto this chaire of state,

And to their painted Arras for a need

From Goodman Usher, or the formall Secretary,   111
Especially the Jugler with the purse,
That paies some shares.   In all, a younger brother, 113
Sometimes an elder, not well trim'd i'th head-
     piece,
May spend what his friends left in expectation,
Oft being turned out of service - for attendance -   116
Or marry a waiting woman, and be damn'd for't   117
To open laughter, and what's worse, old beggerie.   118
What thinkes my <u>Livio</u> of this rise at first?
Is't not miraculous?

     <u>Liv</u>.   It seems the bargaine   120
Was driven before betweene yee.

     <u>Troy</u>.   'Twas, and nothing
Could void it, but the peevish resolution
Of your dissent from goodnesse, as you call it,
A Thin, a threadbare honesty, a vertue
Without a living to't.

     <u>Liv</u>.   I must resolve
To turne my sister whore, speake a homeword,
For my old Batchelor. -- <u>Lord</u>, so, i'st not so?   127
A trifle in respect of present meanes,
Here's all ----

     <u>Troy</u>. Be yet more confident. The slaverie 129
Of such an abject office, shall not tempt

The freedome of thy spirit. Stand ingenious   131
To thine owne fate, and we will practise wisely
Without the charge of scandall.

    <u>Liv.</u>   May it prove so.

                Exit Troylo and Livio   04

[I. ii]

6 Enter Secco with a Castingbottle, sprinckling
        his Hatte and Face, and a little lookeing
        glasse at his Girdle, setting his Counte-
        nance.

    <u>Sec.</u> Admirable! incomparably admirable!
to be the minion, the darling, the delight of
love, 'tis a very tickling to the marrow, a kis-
sing i'th' blood, a bosoming the extasie, the   4
rapture of virginity, soule and paradise of perfection. -- Ah --[Enter Spadone.] pitty of   6
generation <u>Secco</u>, there are no more such men.

    <u>Spa.</u> O yes! If any man, woman, or beast,   8
have found, stolne, or taken up a fine, very fine
male Barber, of the age of above or under eighteene more or lesse.

    <u>Sec.</u> <u>Spadone</u>, hold! What's the noise?   12

    <u>Spa.</u> Umh ---- pay the cryer. I have bin   13
almost lost my selfe in seeking you. Heere's   14

a letter from ----

    Sec. Whom, whom my deare <u>Spadone</u>, whom?

    Spa. Soft and faire. And you be so briefe,   17
I'le returne it whence it came, or looke out a
new owner. O yes.   19

    Sec. Low, low, what dost meane? I'st from   20
the glory of beauty, <u>Morosa</u> the fairest faire?   21
Be gentle to me. Here's a duccat. Speake lowe   22
prethe.

    Spa. Give me one, and take t'other. 'Tis   24
from the party. Golden newes believe it.   25

    Sec. Honest <u>Spadone</u>. Divine <u>Morosa</u>. [Reads]   26

    Spa. [Aside] Fairest faire, quoth a'! So   27
is an old rotten Codled mungrell, parcell Bawde,
parcell midwife. All the markes are quite out   29
of her mouth; not the stumpe of a tooth left in   30
her head to mumble the curd of a Posset. ----   31
Seignior 'tis as I told yee, all's right?   32

    Sec. Right, just as thou tould'st me,   33
all's right.   34

    Spa. To a very haire <u>Seignior mio</u>.

    Sec. For which, Sirrah <u>Spadone</u>, I will   36
make thee a man, a man, dost heare? I say a
man.

7   Spa. Th'art a prickeard foyst, a citterne

headed gew, gaw, a knacke, a snipper-snapper.   40

Twit mee with the decrements of my pendants.   41

Though I am made a gelding, and like a tame

Buck have lost my Dowsets, more a monster then

a Cuckold with his hornes seene, yet I scorne

to be jeer'd by any checker, aproved Barbarian

of yee all. Make me a man! I defie thee.   46

    Sec. How now fellow, how now, roring ripe
indeed.

    Spa. Indeed? Th'art worse, a drie shaver,
a copper basand-suds-monger.

    Sec. Nay, nay, by my Mistresse faire eyes
I meant no such thing.

    Spa. Eyes in thy belly! The reverend Mad-   53
am shall know how I have beene used. I will   54
blow my nose in thy castingbottle, breake the   55
teeth of thy combes, poyson thy camphire Balls,

slice out thy towels with thine owne razor,

betallow thy tweezes, and urine in thy bason.   58

Make me a man?

    Sec. Hold! take another Duccat. As I love   60
new cloathes --   61

    Spa. Or cast old ones.

    Sec. Yes, or cast old ones. I intended   63
no injury.

Spa. Good, we are piec'd againe. Repu-   65
tation, Seignior, is precious.

Sec. I know it is.

Spa. Old sores would not be rub'd.

Sec. For me never.

Spa. The Lady guardianesse, the mother of
the Fancies, is resolved to draw with yee, in
the wholesome of matrimony, suddenly.

Sec. Shee writes as much, and Spadone,
when wee are married --   74

Spa. You will to bed no doubt.

Sec. We will revell in such variety of
delights.

Spa. Doe miracles and get Babies.

Sec. Live so sumptuously.

Spa. In feather and old furres.

8   Sec. Feed so deliciously.

Spa. On Pap and Bulbeefe.

Sec. Enjoy the sweetnes of our yeers.

Spa. Eighteene and threescore with advantage.   84

Sec. Tumble and wallow in aboundance.

Spa. The pure christall puddle of pleasures.

Sec. That all the world should wonder.

Spa. A pox on them that envy yee.

    <u>Sec</u>. How doe the beauties (my dainty
knave) live, wish, thinke, and dreame, sirrah?   91
Ha?

    <u>Spa</u>. Fumble one with an other, on the
gambos of imagination between their legs.   94
Eate they doe, and sleepe, game, laugh, and
lye downe, as beauties ought to doe. There's   96
all.

    <u>Sec</u>. Commend me to my choisest, and tell
her, the minute of her appointment shall be
waited on. Say to her, she shall find me a   100
man <u>at</u> <u>all</u> <u>points</u>.

              Enter Nitido.

    <u>Spa</u>. Why, there's another quarrell, man.   102
Once more in spight of my nose.

    <u>Nit</u>. Away <u>Secco</u>, away! My Lord cals.   104
A' has a loose haire started from his fellowes   105
A clip of your art is commanded.

    <u>Sec</u>. I fly <u>Nitido</u>. <u>Spadone</u> remember me   107

                  Exit Secco.   03

    <u>Nit</u>. Trudging betweene an old moyle, and
a young Calfe, my nimble intelligencer? What,   109

thou fatten'st apace on Capon still?

    <u>Spa</u>. Yes crimpe. 'Tis a gallant life to   111
bee an old Lords <u>pimpe</u> <u>whiskin</u>, but beware of
the porters lodge, for carrying tales out of
the schoole.

    <u>Nit</u>. What a terrible sight to a lib'd
breech is a sow gelder!   116

    <u>Spa</u>. Not so terrible as a crosse tree
that never growes, to a wag-halter-Page.

    <u>Nit</u>. Good! witty rascall. Th'art a Satire   119
I protest, but that the Nimphs need not feare
9 the evidence of thy mortality. Goe put on a   121
cleane bib, and spinne amongst the Nuns! Sing   122
'em a bawdy song. All the children thou get'st   123
shall bee christened in wassaile bowles and
turn'd into a college of <u>men</u> <u>Midwives</u>. Fare-   125
well night-mare.

    <u>Spa</u>. Very,. very well! If I dye in thy   127
debt for this (crackrope) let me be buried in a   128
cole-sacke. I'le fit yee (apes face) looke   129
for't.

    <u>Nit</u>. [Sings] <u>And</u> <u>still</u> <u>the</u> <u>Urchin</u> <u>would</u>, <u>but</u>   131
<u>could</u> <u>not</u> <u>doe</u>.

    <u>Spa</u>. Marke the end on't, and laugh at last.

                    Exit Nitido and Spadone.   04

[I. iii]

                    Enter Romanello and Castamela.

        Rom. Tell me you cannot love me.

        Cas.   You importune   1
Too strict a resolution. As a gentleman   2
Of commendable parts, and faire deserts,
In every sweet condition that becomes
A hopefull expectation, I doe honour
Th' example of your youth, but Sir our fortunes
Concluded on both sides in narrow bands,
Move you to conster gently my forbearance,
In argument of fit consideration.
        Rom. Why, Castamela, I have shapt thy
        vertues   10
(Even from our childish yeeres) into a dowry
Of richer estimation, then thy portion,
Doubled an hundred times, can equall. Now   13
I cleerely find, thy current of affection
Labours to fall into the gulf of riot,   15
Not the free ocean of a soft content.
You'd marry pompe and plenty. 'Tis the Idoll   17
(I must confesse) that creatures of the time,
Bend their devotions to. But I have
        fashion'd   19

Thoughts much more excellent of you.

    <u>Cas</u>. Enjoy your own prosperity. <u>I</u> am re-

    solv'd,   21

Never by any charge with me, to force

A poverty upon yee, want of love.

10 'Tis rarely cherish'd with the love of want.

Ile not be your undoing.

    <u>Rom</u>.   Sure some dotage

Of living stately, richly, lends a cunning   26

To Eloquence. How is this piece of goodnesse

Chang'd to ambition? Oh you are most miserable   28

In your desires. The female curse has caught yee.   29

    <u>Cas</u>. Fie, fie, how il this suits.

    <u>Rom</u>.   A Divell of pride   30

Ranges in airy thoughts to catch a starre,

Whiles yee graspe mole-hils.

    <u>Cas</u>.   Worse and worse I vow.

    <u>Rom</u>. But that some remnant of an honest

    sence   33

Ebbes a full tide of blood to shame, all women

Would prostitute al honour to the luxurie   35

Of ease and titles.

    <u>Cas</u>.   <u>Romanello</u>, know

You have forgot the noblenesse of truth,

And fixt on scandall now.

<u>Rom</u>. A Dogge, a Parrot,

A Monkey, a Caroach, a guarded lackey,

A waiting woman with her lips seald up,

Are pretty toyes to please my Mistresse wanton.   41

So is a fiddle too -- 'twill make it dance,   42

Or else be sicke and whine.

    <u>Cas</u>.   This is uncivill.

I am not Sir your charge.

    <u>Rom</u>.   My griefe you are,

For all my services are lost and ruin'd.

    <u>Cas</u>. So is my chiefe opinion of your wor-

thinesse,

When such distractions tempt yee. You would

    prove   47

A cruell Lord, who dare, being yet a servant,

As you professe, to bait my best respects

Of duty to your welfare. 'Tis a madnesse   50

I have not oft observed. Possesse your freedome.   51

You have no right in me. Let this suffice: 52

I wish your joyes much comfort.

Enter Livio fresh suited.

11   <u>Liv</u>.   Sister, looke yee,

How by a new creation of my Taylors,   54

I've shooke off old mortality. The rags   55

Of home spun Gentry (prethee sister marke it)

Are cast by, and I now appeare in fashion

Unto men, and am receiv'd. Observe me sister --   58

The consequence concernes you.

    <u>Cas</u>.   True good Brother,

For my well doing must consist in yours.

    <u>Liv</u>. Heere's <u>Romanello</u>, a fine temper'd

    gallant,

Of decent carriage, of indifferent meanes,

Considering that his sister, new hoist up   63

From a lost merchants warehouse, to the titles

Of a great Lords-bed, may supply his wants;   65

Not sunck in his acquaintance, for a scholler

Able enough, and one who may subsist

Without the helpe of friends, provided alwayes,

He flie not upon wedlocke without certainty

Of an advancement -- else a batchelor   70

May thrive by observation on a little,   71

As single life's no burthen. But to draw   72

In yoakes is chargeable, and will require

A double maintenance. Why I can live   74

Without a wife, and purchase.

    <u>Rom</u>.   I'st a mysterie   75

Y'ave lately found out <u>Livio</u>, or a cunning

Conceal'd till now for wonder?

    <u>Liv</u>.   Pish, believe it.   77

Endevours and an active braine, are better

Then patrimonies left by parents. Prove it.

One thrives by cheating - shallow fooles and

        unthrifts   80

Are game knaves onely flie at; then a fellow   81

Presumes on his haire, and that his backe can

        toile

12 For fodder from the City - lies; another   83

Reputed valiant lives by the sword, and takes

        up

Quarrels or braves them, as the novice likes,

To build his reputation - most improbable.   86

A world of desperate undertakings, possibly,

Procures some hungry meales, some taverne

        surfets,

Some frippery to hide nakednesse - perhaps   89

The scambling halfe a duccat now and then

to rore and noyse it with the tatling hostesse,

For a weekes lodging. These are pretty shifts,   92

Soules bankerupt of their royalty submit to.

Give me a man, whose practice and experience   94

Conceives not barely the Philosophers stone,

But indeed has it, one whose wit's his Indies.   96

The poore is most ridiculous.

    Rom.   Y'are pleasant

In new discoveries of fortune: use them

With moderation, Livio.

    Cas.   Such wilde language

Was wont to be a stranger to your custome;

How ever, Brother, you are pleas'd to vent it,

I hope, for recreation.

    Liv.   Name and honour.   102

What are they? a meer sound without supportance.   103

A begging chastity, youth, beauty, hansomnesse,

Discourse, behaviour which might charm attention,

And curse the gazers eyes into amazement   106

Are Natures common bounties. So are Diamonds   107

Uncut, so flowers unworne, so silke-wormes webs

Unwrought, gold unrefin'd. Then all those glories   109

are of esteeme, when us'd and set at price.   110

There's no darke sence in this.

    Rom.   I understand not

The drift on't, nor how meant, nor yet to whom.

    Cas. Pray Brother be more plaine.

    Liv.   First Romanello,

13 This for your satisfaction. If you waste   114

More houres in courtship to this maid, my sister,

Weighing her competency with your owne,

You goe about to build without foundation;

So that care will prove void.

    <u>Rom</u>.   A sure acquittance,

If I must be discharged.

    <u>Liv</u>.   Next <u>Castamela</u>,

To thee (my owne lov'd sister) let me say

I have not beene so bountifull, in shewing

To Fame, the treasure, which this age hath open'd   122

As thy true value merits.

    <u>Cas</u>.   You are merry.

    <u>Liv</u>. My jealousie of thy fresh blooming

    yeeres,

Prompted a feare of husbanding too charily

Thy growth to such perfection as no flattery

Of art can perish now.

    <u>Cas</u>.   Here's talke in riddles.

Brother, th' exposition?

    <u>Liv</u>.   I'le no longer

Chamber thy freedome. We have beene already   129

Thrifty enough in our lowe fortunes. Henceforth   130

Command thy liberty, with that thy pleasures.

    <u>Rom</u>. Is't come to this?

    <u>Cas</u>. Y'are wondrous full of curtesie.

    <u>Liv</u>. Ladies of birth and quality are suit-

    ors

For being knowne t'ee. I have promised, sister,   134
They shall partake your company.

    <u>Cas</u>.   What Ladyes?   135
Where, when, how, who?

    <u>Liv</u>.   A day, a weeke, a month
Sported amongst such beauties is a gaine   137
On time. Th'are young, wise, noble, faire, and
    chast.   138

    <u>Cas</u>. Chast?

    <u>Liv</u>. <u>Castamela</u>, chast! I would not hazard   139
My hopes, my joyes of thee, on dangerous triall.

14 Yet if (as it may chance) a neat cloath'd merriment
Passe without blush in tatling so the words   142
Fall not too broad, 'tis but a pastime smil'd at
Amongst your selves in counsaile. But beware   144
Of being over-heard.

    <u>Cas</u>.   This is pretty.

    <u>Rom</u>. [Aside] I doubt I know not what, yet
    must be silent.

Enter Troylo, Floria, Clarella, Silvia and Nitido.   03

    <u>Liv</u>. They come as soon as spoke of. --
Sweetest faire-ones,   147

My sister cannot but conceive this honour

Particular in your respects. Deare sir   149

You grace us in your favours.

    Troy.   Vertuous Lady.

    Flo. We are your servants.

    Cla.   Your sure friends.

    Sil.   Society   151

May fix us in a league.

    Cas.   All fitly welcome.

I find not reason (gentle Ladyes) whereon

To cast this debt of mine, but my acknowledge-

    ment

Shall study to pay thankfulnesse.

    Troy.   Sweet beauty,

Your Brother hath indeed beene too much churle

In this concealement from us all, who love him,

Of such desir'd a presence.

    Sil.   Please to enrich us

With your wish'd amity.

    Flo.   Our coach attends;

We cannot be deny'd.

    Cla.   Command it Nitido.   160

    Nit. Ladies, I shall. [Aside] Now for a

    lusty harvest.   161

'Twill prove a cheap yeare, should these barnes

be fil'd once.

                                        Exit.   04

    <u>Cas</u>.   Brother, one word in private.

    <u>Liv</u>.   [Aside]   Phew ---- anon.   163

15 I shall instruct at large. -- We are prepar'd   164

And easily intreated; 'tis good manners

Not to be troublesome.

    <u>Troy</u>.   Thou art perfect <u>Livio</u>.

    <u>Cas</u>.   [Aside] Whether -- but -- hee's my

brother.

    <u>Troy</u>.   <u>Faire</u>, your arme.

I am your Usher Lady.

    <u>Cas</u>.   As you please sir.

    <u>Liv</u>.   I waite you to your coach.

                           Some two houres hence,   169

I shall returne againe.

                           Exit all but Romanello.   05

    <u>Rom</u>.   <u>Troylo</u>-<u>Savelli</u>,

Next heire unto the marquesse? and the Page too?

The Marquesses owne page, <u>Livio</u> transform'd

Into a suddaine bravery, and alter'd

In Nature, or I dreame? Amongst the Ladies,   174

I not remember I have seene one face.

There's cunning in these changes. I am resolute   176

Or to pursue the trick on't, or lose labour.

                                        Exit.   06

Act II

[II. i]

Enter Flavio supported by Camillo, and Vespuci.

  <u>Fla</u>. Not yet return'd.

  <u>Cam</u>.   Madam.

  <u>Fla</u>.   The Lord our husband,

We meane. Unkind! foure houres are almost past   2

(But twelve short minutes wanting by the glasse)

Since we broke company. Was never (gentlemen)   4

Poore Princesse us'd so?

  <u>Ves</u>.   With your gracious favour,

Peeres great in ranck and place ought of neces-

  sity   6

To attend on state employments.

  <u>Cam</u>. For such duties   7

16 Are all their toyle and labour, but their plea-

  sures

Flow in the beauties they injoy, which conquers

All sence of other travaile.

  <u>Fla</u>.   Trimly spoken.

When we were <u>common</u>, <u>mortall</u>, and a <u>subject</u>,

As other creatures of heavens making are,

(the more the pitty, blesse us) how we waited   13

For the huge play day when the Pageants flutter'd

About the City, for we then were certaine   15

The Madam courtiers would vouchsafe to visit us,   16

And call us by our names, and eate our viands-   17

Nay give us leave to sit at the upper end

of our owne Tables, telling us how welcome

They'd make us, when we came to Court. Full

   little   20

Dream't I at that time of the wind that blew me

Up to the Weathercocke of th'honours now   22

Are thrust upon me. But we beare the burthen,   23

Were't twice as much as'tis. The next great

   feast,   24

Wee'l grace the City wives (poore soules) and

   see

How they'le behave themselves, before our pre-

   sence.

You two shall wait on us.

   Ves.   With best observance,

And glory in our service.

   Cam.   Wee are creatures

Made proud in your commands.

   Fla.   Beleeve't you are so.   29

And you shall find Us readier in your pleasures,

Then you in your obedience. Fie, methinks   31

I have an excellent humor to be pettish,   32

A little toysome. 'Tis a pretty signe   33

Of breeding, i'st not sirs? I could, indeed la,

Long for some strange good things now.

    Cam.   Such newes, Madam,

Would over-joy my Lord your husband.

    Ves.   Cause

Bonfires and bell ringings.

17   Fla.   I must be with childe then,   37

And't be but for the publique Jollity,

Or lose my longings, which were mighty pitty.

    Cam. Sweet fates forbid it.

Enter Fabricio.

    Fab.   Noblest Lady ----

    Ves.   Rudenesse!   40

Keepe off, or I shal! -- Sawcy groome, learn

      manners!   41

Goe swab amongst your Goblins.

    Fla.   Let him stay.   42

The fellow I have seene, and now remember

His name- Fabricio.

    Fab.   Your poore Creature Lady.   44

Out of your gentlenesse, please you to consider

The briefe of this petition, which containes
All hope of my last fortunes.

    <u>Fla</u>.   Give it from him.

    <u>Cam</u>. Here Madam. -- [Cam. and Ves. Aside]

    Marke <u>Vespuci</u>, how the   48
Wittol stares on his <u>sometime</u> <u>wife</u>! Sure he
    imagines   49
To be a cuckold, by consent, is purchase
Of appprobation in a state.

    <u>Ves</u>.   Good reason.
The gaine repriev'd him from bankerouts statute,
And fil'd him in the charter of his freedome.
<u>Shee</u> had seene the <u>fellow</u>, didst observe.

    <u>Cam</u>.   Most punctually,
Could cal him by his name too. Why 'tis possible, 55
Shee has not yet forgot a' was <u>her</u> <u>husband</u>. 56

    <u>Ves</u>. That were strange. Oh 'tis a <u>pre-</u>
    <u>cious</u> <u>trincket</u>.   57
Was ever puppet so slipt up?

    <u>Cam</u>.   The tale
Of <u>Venus</u> <u>Cat</u> (man chang'd into a woman)   59
Was enbleme but to this. She turnes.

    <u>Ves</u>.   A' stands   60
Just like <u>Acteon</u> in the painted cloth.

    <u>Cam</u>.   No more.

<u>Fla</u>. Friend we have read, and weighed the sum

18 Of what your <u>Scrivener</u>, which in effect

Is meant your counsell learned, has drawn for yee.   64

'Tis a faire hand, insooth, but the contents   65

Somewhat unseasonable, for let us tell yee,

Y'ave beene a spender, a vaine spender, wasted

Your stocke of credit, and of Wares unthriftily.

<u>You</u> are a faulty man, and should we urge

<u>Our</u> <u>Lord</u> as often for supplies, as shame,

Or wants drive you to aske, it might be construed

An impudence, which we defie - an Impudence,   72

Base in <u>base</u> <u>Women</u>, but in <u>Noble</u> sinfull.

Are yee not asham'd yet of your selfe?

<u>Fab</u>.   Great Lady,

Of my misfortunes I am asham'd.

<u>Cam</u>. [Aside to Ves.]   So, so,

This jeere twangs roundly. Doe's it not <u>Vespuci</u>?   76

<u>Ves</u>. [Aside to Cam.] Why heere's a Lady

worshipfull.

<u>Fla</u>.   Pray gentlemen,

Retire awhile. <u>This</u> <u>fellow</u> shall resolve   78

Some doubts that stick about me.

<u>Both</u>.   As you please.   79

Exit Camillo and Vespuci. 03

<u>Fla</u>. To thee <u>Fabricio</u> - Oh the change is

        cruell -   80
Since I find some small leisure, I must justifie   81
Thou art unworthy of the name of man.

These holy vowes, which we by bonds of Faith,
Recorded in the register of Truth,
Were kept by me unbroken. No assaults   85
Of gifts of courtship from the great and wanton,   86
No threats, nor sence of poverty (to which
Thy riots had betray'd me) could betray
My warrantable thoughts to impure folly.   89
Why wouldest thou force me miserable?

        Fab.   The scorne
Of rumor is reward enough to brand   91
My lewder actions. 'Twas I thought impossible,   92
A beauty fresh as was your youth, could brooke
19 The last of my decayes.

        Fla.   Did I complaine?
My sleeps between thine arms, were even as sound,
My dreames as harmelesse, my contents as free,
As when the best of plenty crown'd our bride bed.
Amongst some of a meane, but quiet fortune,
Distrust of what they call their owne, or Jeal-
        ousie
Of those whom in their bosomes they possesse
Without controule, begets a selfe unworthinesse;

For which feare, or what is worst, desire,   102

Or paultry gaine, they practise art, and labor to

Pander their own wives - those wives whose in-

    nocence,   104

Stranger to language, spoke obedience onely.   105

And such a wife was Flavia to Fabricio.   106

    Fab. My losse is irrecoverable.

    Fla.   Call not

Thy wickednesse thy losse. Without my knowledge   108

Thou souldst me, and in open court protestedst

A precontract unto another, falsly

To justifie a separation. Wherein   111

Could I offend to be believ'd thy Strumpet,

In best sence an Adulteresse? So conceav'd   113

In all opinions, that I am shooke off,

Even from mine own blood, which although I boast

Not Noble, yet 'twas not meane, for Romanello

Mine onely brother, shunnes me, and abhors

To owne me for his sister.

    Fab.   ·   'Tis confest,

I am the shame of mankind.

    Fla.   I live happy

In this great Lords love, now. But could his

    cunning   120

Have train'd me to dishonour, we had never

Beene sunder'd by th'temptation of his <u>purchase</u>.   122

Introth <u>Fabricio</u>, <u>I</u> am little proud of   123

My unsought honours, and so farre from triumph,

That <u>I</u> am not more foole to such as honour me,   125

20 Then to my selfe, who hate this <u>antique carriage</u>.   126

    <u>Fab</u>. You are an Angell rather to be wor-

shipt,

Then grosly to be talked with.

    <u>Fla</u>.   Keepe those Duccats;

I shall provide you better. 'Twere a bravery,   129

Could you forget <u>the place</u> wherein y'ave ren-

der'd

Your name for ever hatefull.

    <u>Fab</u>.   I will doo't.   131

Doo't, excellentest goodnesse, and conclude   132

My dayes in silent goodnesse.

    <u>Fla</u>.   You may prosper

In <u>Spaine</u>, in <u>France</u>, or elsewhere, as in Italie.

Besides, you are a scholer bred, however

You interrupted study with commerce.   136

Ile think of your supplies. Mean time, pray,

    storm not   137

At my behaviour t'ee. I have forgot acquaintance   138

With mine owne -- keepe your first distance ----

Enter Julio, Camillo, Vespuci.

Camillo. who is neere? Vespuci.   140

    Jul. What, Our Ladies cast familier.

    Fla.   Oh my stomach

Wambles at sight of -- sicke, sicke, I am sicke----

I faint at heart. --Kisse me. Nay prethee

    quickly,   143

Or I shall swoon. -- Y'ave staid a sweet while

    from me.   144

And this companion too. ---- Beshrew him.

    Jul.   Dearest,   145

Thou art my health, my blessing. -- [To Cam. and

    Ves.] Turne the banquerout   146

Out of my dores! -- Sirrah, Ile have thee

    whipt,   147

If thou comst here againe.

    Cam.   Hence, hence you vermine.

                       Exit Fabricio.   05

    Jul. How ist my best of joyes?

    Fla.   Prettily mended.   149

Now we have our owne Lord here. I shall never   150

Endure to spare you long out of my sight.

See what the thing presented.

    Jul.   A petition-   152

21 Belike for some new charity.

    <u>Fla.</u>   We must not

Be troubled with his needs. A <u>wanting</u> <u>creature</u>   154

Is monstruous, is as ominous ---- fie, upon't.

Dispatch the <u>silly</u> <u>Mushroome</u> once for all,

And send him with some pittance out o'th coun-

    trey,

Where we may heare no more of him.

    <u>Jul.</u> Thy will shall stand a law, my <u>Flavia</u>.

    <u>Fla.</u> You have beene

In private with <u>our</u> <u>fellow</u> <u>Peeres</u> now. Sha'not

    we   161

Know how the businesse stands. Sure in som

    countrey,   162

<u>Ladies</u> <u>are</u> <u>privy</u> <u>Counsellors</u>, I warrant yee.   163

Are they not thinke yee? There the <u>land</u> is

    (doubtlesse)   164

Most <u>politickly</u> <u>govern'd</u>; all the <u>women</u>

Weare <u>swords</u> and <u>Breeches</u>, I have heard most

    certainely.   166

Such sights were exc'lent.

    <u>Jul.</u> Th'art a matchlesse pleasure!   167

Noe life is sweet without thee. In my heart   168

Raigne Empresse, and be stil'd thy <u>Julio's</u>

    <u>Soveraigne</u>.

My onely, precious deare.

    <u>Fla</u>.   Wee'l prove no lesse t'ee.   170

                         All Exit.   06

[II. ii]

          Enter Troylo and Livio.

    <u>Troy</u>. Sea sicke a shore still? Thou

    couldst rarely scape   1

A <u>Calenture</u> in a long voyage, <u>Livio</u>,

Who in a short one, and at home, art subject   3

To such faint stomacke qualmes. No cordials

    comfort   4

The businesse of thy thoughts, for ought I see.   5

what ayles thee (<u>man</u>)? Be merry, hang up Jeal-

    ousies.   6

    <u>Liv</u>. Who, I, I jealous? no, no! Heere's

    no cause   7

In this place. 'Tis a nunnerie, a retirement   8

For meditation, all the difference extant

But puzzles onely bare beliefe, not grounds it.   10

Rich services in plate! Soft and faire lodgings,   11

Varieties of recreations, exercise

Of musique in all changes? Neate attendance?   13

22 Princely, nay royall furniture of garments?

Satiety of gardens, orchards, waterworkes?   15

Pictures so ravishing, that ranging eyes   16
Might dwell upon a dotage of conceit,
Without a single wish for livelier substance?
The great world in a little world of <u>Fancie</u>   19
Is here abstracted. Noe temptation profer'd   20
But such as <u>fooles</u> and <u>mad</u> <u>folkes</u> can invite to?
And yet ----

    <u>Troy</u>. And yet your reason cannot answer
Th'objections of your feares, which argue danger.

    <u>Liv</u>. Danger? dishonour, <u>Troylo</u>! Were my
    sister   24
In safety from those charmes, I must confesse
I could live here for ever.

    <u>Troy</u>.   But you could not.
<u>I</u> can assure yee, for't were then scarce possi-
    ble   27
A dore might open t'ee, hardly a loope-hole.

    <u>Liv</u>. My presence then is usher to her
    ruine,
And losse of her, the fruit of my preferment.

    <u>Troy</u>. Briefly partake a secret, but be sure
To lodge it in the inmost of thy bosome,
Where memory may not find it for discovery.   33
By our firme truth of friendship, <u>I</u> require
    thee.

<u>Liv</u>. By our firme truth of friendship,

<u>I</u> subscribe

To just conditions.

<u>Troy</u>.   Our great <u>Uncle</u> <u>Marquesse</u>,

Disabled from his Cradle, by an impotence

In nature first, that impotence, since seconded

And rendred more infirme by a fatall breach   39

Receiv'd in fight against the Turkish Gallies,   40

Is made uncapable of any faculty   41

Of active manhood, more then what affections

Proper unto his Sex must else distinguish;   43

So that no helpes of art can warrant life,

Should he transcend the bounds his weaknes limits.

<u>Liv</u>. On, <u>I</u> attend with eagernesse.

23   <u>Troy</u>.   'Tis strange,

Such naturall defects at no time checks

A full and free sufficiency of spirit,   48

Which flowes, both in so cleare and fixt a

        strength,

That to confirme beliefe (it seemes) where na-

        ture

Is in the body lame, she is suppli'd

In fine proportion of the minde. A word   52

Concludes all. To a man his enemy,   53

He is a dangerous threatning, but to women,   54

How ever pleasurable, no way cunning

To shew abilities of friendship, other

Then what his outward sences can delight in,

Or charge and bounty court with.

     Liv.   Good, good ---- Troylo!   58

Oh that I had a lusty Faith to credit it,

Though none of all this wonder should be pos-

     sible.

     Troy. As I love honour, and an honest

     name,

I faulter not (my Livio) in one sillable.   62

     Liv. Newes admirable! 'Tis, 'tis so. --

     Pish I know it!   63

Yet a' has a kind heart of his owne to girles,   64

Young, handsome Girles; yes, yes, so a' may.   65

Tis granted -- a' wod now and then be pidling,

And play the wanton, like a flie that dallies

About a candles flame; then scorch his wings,   68

Drop downe, and creepe away, ha?

     Troy.   Hardly that too.   69

To looke upon fresh beauties, to discourse

In an unblushing merriment of words,

To heare them play or sing, and see them dance,

To passe the time in pretty amorous questions,

Read a chast verse, of love, or prattle riddles,

Is th' height of his temptations.

    <u>Liv</u>.   Send him joy on't.

    <u>Troy</u>. His choices are not of the courtly

    trayne,   76

Nor C{itties practice; but the countries inno-

    cence,

such as are gentle-borne, not meanely; such   78

24 To whom both gawdinesse and apelike fashions

Are monstrous; such as cleanelinesse and de-

    cency   80

Prompt to a vertuous envy; such as study   81

A knowledge of no danger, but themselves.

    <u>Liv</u>. Well, I have liv'd in ignorance.

    The ancients,   83

Who chatted of the golden age, fain'd trifles.

Had they dream't this, they would have truth'd

    it heaven.

I meane an earthly heaven, lesse it is not.

    <u>Troy</u>. Yet is this Batchelor miracle not

    free

From the epidemical head-ach.

    <u>Liv</u>.   The Yellowes?   88

    <u>Troy</u>. Huge jealous fits, admitting none

    to enter

But me, his page, and Barber, with an Eunuch,

And an old guardianesse. It is a favour   91
Not common, that the licence of your visits,
To your owne sister, now and then is wink't at.
    <u>Liv</u>. But why are you his instrument, his
    Nephew?
'Tis ominous in nature.
    <u>Troy</u>.   Not in policy.
Being his heire, I may take truce a little   96
With mine owne fortunes.
    <u>Liv</u>.   Knowing how things stand too.
    <u>Troy</u>. At certaine seasons, as the humor
    takes him,
A set of musicians are permitted peaceably,   99
To cheare their solitarinesse, provided
Th'are strangers, not acquainted neere the city. 101
But never the same twice, pardon him that.   102
Nor must their stay exceed an houre, or two
At farthest, as at this wise wedding. Wherfore   104
His Barber is the master to instruct
The lasses both in Song and Dance, by him
Train'd up in either quality.
    <u>Liv</u>. A caution happily studied.
    <u>Troy</u>.   Farther to prevent
Suspition, a'has married his young Barber
To the old Matron, and withall is pleased.

25 Report should mutter him a mighty man

For th'game, to take off all suspition

Of insufficiency. And this strickt company   113

A' cals his bower of <u>Fancies</u>.

    <u>Liv</u>.   Yes and properly,

Since all his recreations are in <u>Fancy</u>.

I'me infinitely taken. ---- Sister? marry   116

Would I had sisters in a plenty, <u>Troylo</u>,

So to bestow them all, and turne them <u>Fancies</u>.

<u>Fancies</u>? Why 'tis a pretty name methinks.

    <u>Troy</u>. Something remaines, which in con-

clusion shortly   120

<u>Song</u>.

Shall take thee fuller. -- Harke, the wedding

jollity!   121

With a Bride-cake on my life, to grace the

nuptials!

Perhaps the Ladies will turne Songsters.

    <u>Liv</u>.   Silence.

Enter Secco, Castamela, Floria, Clarella, Silvia,

Morosa, and Spadone.

Sec. Passing neat and exquisite. I pro-   124
test faire creatures. These honours to our solem-   125
nity are liberall and uncommon. My spouse and my   126
selfe with our posterity, shall prostitute our
services, to your bounties. Shals not duckling?   128

Mor. Yes <u>honey</u> <u>suckle</u>, and doe as much for
them one day, if things stand right as they should
stand. Bill, Pigeon doe. Thou'st be my <u>Catta-</u>   131
<u>mountaine</u>, and I thy sweet bryer, Honey. Wee'l   132
lead you to kind examples (pretty ones) believe
it. And you shall find us, one in one, whiles   134
hearts doe last.

    Sec. Ever mine owne, and ever.

    Spa. Well said old <u>Touch</u> <u>hole</u>.

    Liv. All happinesse, all joy.

    Troy.   A plenteous issue,
A fruitfull wombe! ---- Thou hast a blessing
    Secco.   139

    Mor. Indeed a' has Sir, if yee know all,   140
as I conceive you know enough, if not the whole.   141
26 For you have (I may say) tryed me to the quick,
through and through, and most of my carriage -   143
from time to time.

    Spa. [Aside] 'Twould wind-breake a moyle,
or a ring'd mare, to vie burthens with her.

<u>Mor</u>. What's that you mumble, Gelding,

shey?   148

<u>Spa</u>. Nothing forsooth, but that y'are a
bouncing couple well met, and 'twere pitty to
part yee, though you hung together in a smoakie
chimney.

    <u>Mor</u>. 'Twere eene pitty indeed, <u>Spadone</u>.   153
Nay th'ast a foolish loving nature of thine own,   154
and wishest wel to plaine dealings o' my conscience.

    <u>Spa</u>. Thank your Brideship -- your Bawdship.

    <u>Flo</u>. Our sister is not merry.

    <u>Cla</u>.   Sadnesse cannot
Become a Bridall harmony.

    <u>Sil</u>.   At a wedding,   158
Free spirits are required.

    <u>Troy</u>.   You should dispence
With serious thoughts now, Lady.   160

    <u>Mor</u>. Well said Gentlefolks.

    <u>Liv</u>.   Fie <u>Castamela</u>! fie!   161

    <u>All</u>. A dance, a dance.   162

    <u>Troy</u>. By any meanes! The day is not com-
pleat else.   163

    <u>Cas</u>. Indeed Ile be excus'd.

    <u>Troy</u>.   By no meanes, Lady.   164

    <u>Sec</u>. We are all suitors.

    <u>Cas</u>.   With your pardons, spare me

For this time. Grant me licence to looke on.   166

    <u>Troy</u>. Command your pleasures, Lady. ----

Every one hand   167

Your Partner. -- Nay, <u>Spadone</u> must make one.   168

These merriments are free.

    <u>Spa</u>.   With all my heart.   169

I'me sure I am not the heaviest in the company.   170

    <u>Troy</u>. Strike up for the honour of the

Bride and Bridegroome.   171

                <u>Dance</u>.   04

So, so, here's art in motion. On all

    parts,   172

Yee have bestir'd yee nimbly.

27   <u>Mor</u>.   I could dance now,   173

Eene till I dropt againe; but want of practice

Denies the scope of breath or so. Yet sirrah,   175

My <u>Cattamountaine</u>, doe not I trip quickly,

And with a grace too, sirrah?

    <u>Sec</u>.   Light as a feather.   177

    <u>Spa</u>. Sure you are not without a stick of

Licorice in your pocket forsooth. You have I   179

believe stout lungs of your owne. You swim   180

about so roundly without rubs. 'Tis a tickling   181

sight to be young still.

                    Enter Nitido.

        Nit. Madam <u>Morosa</u>?

        Mor. Childe.

        Nit. To you in secret.

        Spa. [Aside] That eare-wig scatters the

troope now. Ile goe neer to fit 'em.   187

        Liv. My Lord upon my life.

        Troy.   Then we must sever.

        Mor. Ladies and gentlemen, your eares.

        Spa. [Aside to Sec.] Oh 'twas ever a

wanton monkey---a' will wriggle into a <u>starting</u>

<u>hole</u> so cleanely -- and it had bin on my wedding

day.--- I know what I know.   193

        Sec. Saist so <u>Spadone</u>?

        Spa. Nothing, nothing! I prate sometimes   195

beside the purpose. Whoreson lecherous weezill?   196

        Sec. Looke, looke, looke how officious the

little knave is ---- but ----

        Spa. Why? there's the businesse. <u>Buts</u> on   199

ones forehead, are but scurvie <u>Buts</u>.

    <u>Mor</u>. <u>Spadone</u>, discharge the fidlers

    instantly.

    <u>Spa</u>. Yes, I know my postures -Oh monstruous   203

<u>Buts</u>.

                                   Exit Spadone. 06

    <u>Mor</u>. Attend within, Sweeting. ---- Your

    pardons   205

Gentlemen. To your recreations deare virgins.   206

Page have a care.

    <u>Nit</u>.   My duty reverend Madam.   207

    <u>Troy</u>. <u>Livio</u> away. ----Sweet beauties.

    <u>Cas</u>.   Brother.   208

28   <u>Liv</u>. Suddenly I shall returne. [Aside] Now for

    a round temptation.   209

                      Exit all but Mor. and Cas. 07

    <u>Mor</u>. One gentle word in private with your

    Ladiship.   210

I shal not hold you long.

    <u>Cas</u>.   What meanes this huddle   211

Of flying severall wayes thus? Who has frighted

    'em?   212

They live not at devotion here, or pension!

Pray quit me of distrust.

    <u>Mor</u>.   May it please your <u>Goodnesse</u>,

You'l find him even in every point as honourable,

As flesh and bloud can vouch him.

    <u>Cas</u>.   Ha, him? Whom?   216

What him?

    <u>Mor</u>. He will not presse beyond his bounds.

He will but chat and toy, and feele your ----

    <u>Cas</u>.   Guard me,

A powerfull <u>Genius</u>! Feele ----

    <u>Mor</u>.   Your hands to kisse them.   219

Your faire, pure, white hands- what strange bus-

    inesse is it?   220

These melting twins of Ivory, but softer

Then downe of Turtles, shall but feede the ap-

    petite ----

    <u>Cas</u>. A rape upon my eares.

    <u>Mor</u>.   The appetite

Of his poore ravisht eye. Should he swell higher   224

In his desires, and soare upon ambition

Of rising in humility, by degrees,   226

Perhaps a' might crave leave to clap ----

    <u>Cas</u>.   Fond woman,

In thy grave sinfull.

    <u>Mor</u>.   Clap or pat the dimples,

Where <u>Loves</u> <u>tombe</u> stands erected on your cheekes.

Else pardon those slight exercises, <u>pretty</u> <u>one</u>.   230

His Lordship is as harmelesse a weake implement,

As ere young Lady trembled under.

    <u>Cas</u>.   Lordship!

(Stead me my modest anger) 'tis belike then

29 (Religious matron) some great mans prison,   234

Where Virgins honours suffer Martyrdome.

And you are their tormentor. Let's lay downe   236

Our ruin'd names to the insulters mercy!

Let's sport and smile on scandall. (Rare cal-

    amity,   238

What hast thou toyl'd me in?) You nam'd his

    Lordship -   239

Some gallant youth and fiery?

    <u>Mor</u>.   No, no deed la.

A very grave stale Batchelor (<u>my</u> <u>dainty</u> <u>one</u>) -   241

There's the conceit. Hee's none of your hot

    rovers,   242

Who ruffle at first dash, and so disfigure

Your <u>Dresses</u>, and your sets of blush at once.

Hee's wise in yeeres, and of a temperate warmth;

Mighty in meanes and power, and withall liberall.   246

A wanton in his wishes, but else, farther,

A' cannot ---- cause ---- a' cannot.

    <u>Cas</u>.   Cannot? Prethee,   248

Be plainer. I begin to like thee strangely.   249

What cannot?

    Mor.   You urge timely, and to purpose.

A' cannot doe -- the truth is truth -- doe, any

    thing,

(As one should say) that's any thing, put case

(I doe but put the case forsooth) a' find yee.

    Cas. [Aside] My stars I thank yee, for

    being ignorant,

Of what this old in mischiefe can intend.

And so we might be merry, bravely merry.

    Mor. You hit it -- what else.--[Aside]

    She is cunning. -- Looke yee,   257

Pray lend your hand forsooth.

    Cas.   Why prethee take it.

    Mor. You have a delicate moyst palme. --

    Umh -- can yee   259

Rellish that tickle? There

    Cas.   And laugh if need were.   260

    Mor. And laugh, why now you have it. What

    hurt pray   261

Perceive yee? there's all, all. Goe to, you

    want tutoring;   262

Are an apt scholar. Ile neglect no paines   263

For your instruction.

30   Cas.   Doe not. But his Lordship,   264

What may his <u>Lordship</u> be?

    <u>Mor</u>.   No worse man

Then marquesse of <u>Siena</u>, the great Master

Of this small familie. Your brother found him   267

A bounteous benefactor, has advanc'd him   268

The gentleman o'th horse. In a short time   269

He meanes to visit you <u>himselfe</u> in <u>person</u>,

As kind, as loving, an old man.

    <u>Cas</u>.   Wee'l meet him

With a full flame of welcome. I'st the Marquesse? 272

No worse?

    <u>Mor</u>. No worse I can assure your Ladiship; 273

The onely free maintainer of <u>the</u> <u>Fancies</u>.

    <u>Cas</u>. <u>Fancies</u>? How meane yee that?

    <u>Mor</u>.   The pretty soules   275

Who are companions in the house, all daughters

To honest vertuous parents, and right worship-

    full.

A kind of <u>chaste</u> <u>collapsed</u> <u>Ladies</u>.

    <u>Cas</u>. Chast too, and yet <u>collapsed</u>?

    <u>Mor</u>.   Onely in their fortunes.

    <u>Cas</u>. Sure I must be a <u>Fancie</u> in the number.

    <u>Mor</u>. <u>A</u> <u>Fancie</u> <u>principall</u>! I hope you'le

    fashion   281

Your entertainment, when the Marquesse courts you,

As that I may stand blamelesse.

Cas. Free suspition. My Brothers rayser?

Mor.   Meerely.

Cas. My supporter?

Mor.   Undoubtedly.

Cas.   An old man and a lover?

Mor. True, there's the Musick, the content,

the harmony.

Cas. And I my selfe a Fancy?

Mor.   You are pregnant.

Cas. The chance is throwne; I now am for-

tunes minion.   288

I will be bold and resolute.

Mor.   Blessing on thee.

                    Exit Morosa and Castamela.   08

[III. i]

                    Enter Romanello.

    <u>Rom</u>. Prosper me now my fate; some better
    <u>genius</u>
Then such a one, as waits on troubled passions,
Direct my courses to a noble issue.
My thoughts have wander'd in a labyrinth,
But if the clew I have laid hold on, faile not,
I shall tred out the toyle of these darke paths
In spight of politique reaches. -- I am punish'd   7
In mine owne hopes, by her unluckie fortunes,
Whose fame is ruin'd- <u>Flavia</u>, my lost sister!   9
Lost to report, by her unworthy husband,
Though hightned by a greatnes, in whose mix-
        tures,
I hate to claime a part. ----

                    Enter Nitido.

                        Oh welcome, welcome,   12

Deere boy! thou keep'st time with my expectations

As justly, as the promise of my bounties

Shall reckon with thy service.

    <u>Nit</u>.   I have fashion'd   15

The meanes of your admittance.

    <u>Rom</u>.   Pretious <u>Nitido</u>.

    <u>Nit</u>. More, have bethought me of a shape,

    a quaint one,

You may appeare in, safe and unsuspected.

    <u>Rom</u>. Th'art an ingenious boy.

    <u>Nit</u>.   Beyond all this,   19

Have so contriv'd the feate, that at first sight,

<u>Troylo</u> himselfe shall court your entertainment:

May, force you to vouchsafe it.

    <u>Rom</u>.   Th'ast out done   22

All counsaile, and all cunning.

    <u>Nit</u>.   True, I have sir

Fadg'd nimbly in my practises; but surely,   24

There are some certaine clogs, some roguish

    staggers,

Somewhat shall I call 'em in the busines?

    <u>Rom</u>.   <u>Nitido</u>,   26

32 What faint now? deare heart beare up. What

    staggers,   27

What clogs? Let me remove 'em.

    <u>Nit</u>.   Am I honest   28
In this discovery?

    <u>Rom</u>.   Honest, pish is that all?
By this rich purse, and by the twenty ducats
Which line it, I will answer for thy honesty,
Against all <u>Italie</u>, and prove it perfect.
Besides, remember, I am bound to secresie.
Thou't not betray thy selfe.

    <u>Nit</u>.   All feares are clear'd then.
But if ----

    <u>Rom</u>.   If what? out with't.

    <u>Nit</u>.   If w'are discover'd,
You'le answer I am honest still?

    <u>Rom</u>.   Dost doubt it?

    <u>Nit</u>. Not much; I have your purse in pawne
    for't.   37
Now to the shape. You know the wits in <u>Florence</u>.   38
Who in the great Dukes court, buffoones his com-
    plement,
According to the change of meates in season,
At every free Lords table.

    <u>Rom</u>.   Or free meetings
In Tavernes, there a' sits at the upper end,
And eates, and prates, a' cares not how nor what.
The very quack of fashions, the very <u>hee</u> that   44

Weares a <u>Steletto</u> on his chinne.

    <u>Nit</u>.   You have him.

Like such a thing must you appeare, and study

amongst the Ladies in a formall foppery,

To vent some curiosity of language,

Above their apprehensions, or your owne.   49

Indeed beyond sence, you are the more <u>the</u> <u>person</u>.

Now amorous, then scurvie, sometimes bawdy,

<u>The</u> <u>same</u> <u>man</u> still, but evermore phantasticall,

As being the <u>suppositor</u> <u>to</u> <u>laughter</u>.   53

It hath sav'd charge in physick.

33   <u>Rom</u>.   When occasion

Offers it selfe (for where it do's or not,

I will be bold to take it) I may turne

To some one in the company; and changing

My Method talke of state, and rayle against

Th'imployment of the <u>time</u>, mislike the carriage

Of places, and mislike that men of parts,

Of merit, such as my selfe am, are not

Thrust into <u>publike</u> <u>action</u>. 'Twill set off   62

A privilege I challenge from opinion,

With a more lively current.

    <u>Nit</u>.   On my Modesty,

You are some kin to him ---- Seignior <u>Prugnioli</u>!

Seignior <u>Mushrumpo</u>!

Leape but into his anticke garbe, and trust me,   67
You'le fit it to a thought.

    <u>Rom.</u>   The time?

    <u>Nit.</u>   As suddenly

As you can be transform'd, ---- for the event   69
'Tis pregnant.

    <u>Rom.</u>   Yet my pretty knave, thou hast not
Discover'd where faire <u>Castamela</u> lives;
Nor how, nor amongst whome.

    <u>Nit.</u>   Pish, yet more <u>Queres?</u>   72
Till your owne eyes informe, be silent! Else   73
Take backe your earnest. What, turne woman?

    Fie!   74
Be idle and inquisitive?

    <u>Rom.</u>   No more.
I shall be speedily provided. Aske for   76
A note at mine owne lodging.

                    Exit Romanello.   03

    <u>Nit.</u>   Ile not fayle yee,
Assuredly, I wil not fayle you Seignior.   78
My fine <u>inamorato</u> ---- twenty ducats?
Th'are halfe his quarters income. ---- Love,

    oh love,   80
What a pure madnesse art thou? I shall fit him,
Fit, quit and split him too -- most bounteous

sir.

34   Enter Troylo.

    Troy. Boy, thou art quicke and trustie.   83
Be withall close and silent, and thy paines
Shall meet a liberall addition.
    Nit.   Though sir,
I'me but a child, yet you shall find me ----
    Troy.   Man   86
In the contrivements; I will speake for thee.
Well a' does relish the disguise!
    Nit.   Most greedily   88
Swallowes it with a licourish delight.   89
Will instantly be shap't in't, instantly.
And on my conscience, sir, the supposition
Strengthned by supposition, will transforme him
Into the beast it selfe a' do's resemble.   93
    Troy. Spend that, and looke for more boy.
    Nit.   Sir, it needs not;   94
I have already twenty Ducats pursed
In a gay case. 'Las sir, to you, my service   96
Is but my duty.
    Troy.   Modestie in Pages

Shews not a vertue, boy, when it exceeds

Good manners.   Where must we meet?

  <u>Nit</u>.   Sir at's lodging,

Or neere about.   He will make haste, beleeve

  it.   100

  <u>Troy</u>.   Waite th' opportunity, and give me

  notice.

I shall attend.

  <u>Nit</u>.   If I miss my part, hang me.

         Exit Troylo and Nitido. 05

[III. ii]

     Enter Vespuci and Camillo.

  <u>Ves</u>.   Come th'art caught <u>Camillo</u>.

  <u>Cam</u>.   Away, away,

That were a jest indeed.   I caught?

  <u>Ves</u>.   The Lady 2

Does scatter glances, wheeles her round, and

  smiles;

Steales an occasion to aske how the minutes

35 Each houre have runne in progresse; then, thou

  kissest

All thy foure fingers, crowchest and sighst

  faintly:

<u>Deare beauty</u>, if my watch keep faire <u>decorum</u>,

Three quarters have neere past the figure X.

Or as the time of day goes ----

    <u>Cam</u>.   So <u>Vespuci</u>,

This will not doe. I reade it on thy forehead;   10

The graine of thy complexion is quite altered.

Once 'twas a comely browne, 'tis now of late

A perfect greene and yellow; sure prognosticates

Of th' over flux o'th gall, and <u>melancholy</u>,

Symptomes of <u>love</u> and <u>jealousie</u>, poore soule.

Quoth <u>she</u>, the <u>she</u>, why hang thy looks like bel-

      ropes

Out of the wheeles? Thou flinging downe thy eyes   17

Low at her feete, replid'st: Because, oh <u>Sov</u>-

      <u>eraigne</u>,   18

The <u>great</u> <u>bell</u> of my <u>heart</u> is crack'd, and never

Can ring in tune againe, till't be new cast

By one only skilfull Foundresse. ---- Hereat   21

She turn'd aside, wink'd; thou stood'st still

      and stard'st.   22

I did observ't. Be plaine, what hope?

    <u>Ves</u>.   Shee loves thee;   23

Doates on thee. In my hearing told her Lord   24

<u>Camillo</u> was the <u>Piramus</u> and <u>Thisbe</u>

Of courtship, and of complement. Ah ha!   26

<u>She</u> nick'd it there. I envy not thy fortunes;

For to say truth, th'art hansome, and deserv'st

her,

Were she as great againe as she is.

    Cam.   I hansome?

Alas, alas, a creature of heavens making,

Ther's all! But sirrah, prithee let's be so-

    ciable.   31

I doe confesse, I think the goodee-madame

May possibly be compost; I resolve too,

To put in for a share- come what can come on't.   34

    Ves. A pretty toy 'tis. Since th'art open

    brested,   35

Camillo, I presume she is wanton,   36

And therefore meane to give the sowse, when ever

36 I find the game on wing.

    Cam.   Let us consider,

Shee's but a merchants leavings.

    Ves.   Hatch'd i'th countrey,

And fledg'd i'th City.

    Cam.   'Tis a common custome

'Mongst friends (they are not friends else)

    chiefly gallants,

To trade by turnes in such like fraile commod-

    ities.

The one is but reversioner to t'other.   43

    Ves. Why 'tis the fashion man.

    <u>Cam</u>.   Most free and proper,

One Surgeon, one apothecarie.

    <u>Ves</u>.   Thus then,   45

When I am absent, use the gentlest memory

Of my endowments, my unblemish't services

To Ladies favours: with what Faith and secresie,

I live in her commands, whose speciall curtesies,

Oblige me to particular engagements

Ile doe as much for thee.

    <u>Cam</u>.   With this addition: 51

<u>Camillo</u> (<u>best</u> <u>of</u> <u>faires</u>) a man so bashfull,

So simply harmeless, and withall so constant,

Yet resolute in all true rights of honour,   54

That to deliver him in perfect character,

Were to detract from such a solid vertue

As raignes not in another soule. -- He is   57

    <u>Ves</u>. The thing a <u>Mistresse</u> ought to wish

    her servant.   58

Are we agreed?

    <u>Cam</u>.   Most readily. On t'other side,   59

Unto the Lord her husband, talke as coursely

Of one another as we can.

    <u>Ves</u>.   I like it.   61

So shall we sift her love, and his opinion.

Enter Julio, Flavia, and Fabricio.   02

Jul. Be thankfull (fellow) to a noble

Mistresse;

Two hundred ducats are no trifling summe,

37 Nor common almes.

Fla.   You must not loyter lazily,

And speake about the towne my friend in tavernes,

In gaming houses, nor sneake after dinner

To publike shewes, to interludes, in riot,

To some lewd painted baggage, trick't up gawdily,

Like one of us. Oh fie upon 'em giblets!   70

I have bin told they ride in coaches, flaunt it

In braveries, so rich, that it is scarce possible

How to distinguish one of these vile naughty packs,

From true and arrant Ladies. -- They'le inveigle   74

Your substance and your body, thinke on that!   75

I say your body, looke to't.

Is't not sound counsell?

Jul.   'Tis more, 'tis heavenly.

Ves. [Aside to Cam.] What hope Camillo

now if this tune hold?

Cam. [Aside to Ves.] Hope faire enough,

Vespuci, now as ever.   79

Why any Woman in her husbands presence

Can say no less.

    <u>Ves</u>. [Aside to Cam.] 'Tis true, and she

hath leave here.   81

    <u>Fab</u>. Madam, your care and charity at once,

Have so new moulded my resolves,

That henceforth when e're my mention fals into

report,   84

It shall requite this bounty. I am travelling   85

To a new world.

    <u>Jul</u>.   I like your undertakings.

    <u>Fla</u>. New world? Where's that I pray?

    Good, if you light on   87

A Parrot or a Monkey that has qualities

Of a new fashion, thinke on me.

    <u>Fab</u>.   Yes, Lady

I, I shall thinke on you; and my devotions

Tendred where they are due in single meekenes,

With purer flames will mount with free increase

Of plenty, honors, full contents, full blessings,

Truth and affection twixt your Lord and you.

38 So with my humblest best leave, I turne from you.

Never as now I am to appeare before yee.

All joyes dwell here and lasting.

                    Exit Fabricio.   03

    <u>Fla</u>.   Prithee <u>sweetest</u>,   97

Harke in your eare.---- Beshrew't, the brim of

    your hat   98.

Strucke in mine eye. -- [Aside] Dissemble honest

    teares   99

The griefes my heart does labour in ---- smarts

Unmeasurably.

    Jul.   A chance, a chance, 'twill off, 101

Suddenly off. Forbeare, this handkercher   102

But makes it worse.

    Cam.   Wincke madam with that eye.   103

The paine will quickly passe.

    Ves.   Immediatly,

I know it by experience.

    Fla.   Yes, I find it.

    Jul. Spare us a little Gentlemen.

                Exit Camillo and Vespuci.   04

                    Speak freely.   106

What wer't thou saying deerest?

    Fla.   Doe you love me?

Answer in sober sadnesse, I'me your wife now;

I know my place and power.

    Jul.   What's this riddle?

Thou hast thy selfe reply'd to thine owne ques-

    tion,

In being marryed to me- a sure argument   111

Of more than protestation.

    <u>Fla</u>.   Such it should be

Were you as other husbands. 'Tis granted,   113

A woman of my state may like good cloaths,

Choyce dyet, many servants, change of merriments;   115

All these I doe enjoy- and wherefore not?   116

<u>Great</u> <u>Ladies</u> should command their owne delights,

And yet for all this, I am us'd but homely,

But I am serv'd even well enough.

    <u>Jul</u>.   My <u>Flavia</u>

I understand not what thou would'st.

    <u>Fla</u>.   Pray pardon me;   120

39 I doe confesse I'm foolish, very foolish;

Trust me indeed I am, for I could cry

Mine eyes out, being in the weeping humour.   123

You know I have a Brother.

    <u>Jul</u>.   <u>Romanello</u>,

An unkinde Brother.

    <u>Fla</u>.   Right, right, since you bosom'd

My latter youth, he never would vouchsafe

As much as to come neere me. Oh, it made me,

Being but two, that we should live at distance,   128

As if I were a Cast-away; and you   129

For your part take no care on't, nor attempt   130

To draw him hither.

    <u>Jul.</u>   Say the man be peevish,

Must I petition him?

    <u>Fla.</u>   Yea marry must ye,

Or else you love not me. Not see my Brother?   133

Yes I will see him, so I will, will see him.

You hear't. ---- Oh my good Lord, deere gentle,

    prethee,   135

You shan't be angrie. 'Las I know poore Gentle-

    man,   136

A' beares a troubled mind, but let us meete   137

And talke a little; we perhaps may chide   138

At first, shed some few teares, and then be quiet. 139

There's all.

    <u>Jul.</u>   Write to him, and invite him hither,

Or goe to him thy selfe. Come, no more sadnesse,

Ile doe what thou canst wish.

    <u>Fla.</u>   And in requitall,

Beleeve I shall say something that may settle

A constancie of peace, for which thou'lt

    thanke me.   144

                      Exit Flavia and Julio. 05

[III. iii]

                Enter Secco and Spadone.

    <u>Sec.</u> The rarest fellow, <u>Spadone</u>, so full

of gamballs. A' talkes so humorously, does a'   2

not, so carelessely? Oh rich! O, my hope of   3

posterity! I could be in love with him.

    Spa. His tongue troules like a Mill-clack.   5

a' towzes the Lady sisters, as a tumbling Dog   6

does young Rabets- hey here, dab there! Your   7

Madona, a' has a catch at her too. There's a   8

tricke in the businesse; I am a dunce else. I   9

say a shrewd one.

    Sec. Jumpe with me. I smell a trick too,   11

if I could tell what.

    Spa. Who brought him in? That would be   13

knowne?

    Sec. That did Signior Troylo; I saw the   15

Page part at the doore. Some trick still, go to   16

Wife. I must and I will have an eye to this   17

geere.

    Spa. A plaine case- Roguery, Brokage and   19

Roguery, or call me Bulchin. Fancies, quoth

a'? Rather Frenzies. We shall all rore shortly: 21

turne madcaps, lie open to what comes first. I   22

may stand to't. That boy Page, is a naughty boy   ·

Page. Let me feele your forehead. Ha, oh, hum,   24

- yes- there, - there againe; I'm sorry for ye;   25

a hand-saw cannot cure ye, monstrous and appar-

ent.

    Sec. What, what, what, what, what <u>Spadone</u>?

    Spa. What what what what, nothing but

Velvet tips. You are of the first head yet.   30

Have a good hart man. A Cuckold though a' be a   31

Beast, weares invisible hornes; else we might   32

not know a City Bull from a Countrey Calfe,----

villanous Boy still.

    Sec. My Razer shall be my weapon, my Razer.

    Spa. Why? Hee's not come to the honour of   36

a Beard yet; he needs no shaving.   37

    Sec. I will trim him and tram him.

    Spa. Nay, she may doe well enough for one.   39

    Sec. One, ten, a hundred, a thousand, ten   40

thousand: doe beyond Arithmetick <u>Spadone</u>. I   41

speake it with some passion; I am a notorious   42

Cuckold.

    Spa. Grosse and ridiculous!---- Look ye,   44

point blanck I dare not sweare that this same

Mountbancking newcome foyst, is at least a pro-   46

curer in the businesse; if not a pretender him-

selfe. But I thinke what I thinke.   48

    Sec. Hee, <u>Troylo</u>, <u>Livio</u>, the Page, that

hole-creeping Page- all horne me sirrah; Ile   50

41 forgive thee from my heart- Dost not thou   51

drive a trade too in my bottome?   52

   Spa. A likely matter- 'las I'm Metamor-   53

phosed I. Be patient. You'l marre all else.   54

       <u>Within</u>. Ha ha ha ha.

   <u>Sec</u>. Now, now, now, now, the games rampant,

rampant.

   <u>Spa</u>. Leave your wild fegaries, and learne

to be a tame Antick, or Ile observe no longer.

       <u>Within</u>. Ha ha ha ha.

Enter Troylo, Castamela, Floria, Clarella, Sil-   02

  via, Morosa, and Romanello, like a Courtly

  Mountebanck.

   <u>Sil</u>. You are extremely busie signior.

   <u>Flo</u>.   Courtlie,

Without a fellow.

   <u>Cla</u>.   Have a stabbing wit.

   <u>Cas</u>. But are you alwaies, when you presse

  on Ladies

Of mild and easie nature, so much satyre;

So tart and keen as we doe taste ye now?

It argues a leane braine.

Rom.   Gip to your beauties.   66

You would be faire. Forsooth, you would be

Monsters;   67

Faire Women are such. Monsters to bee seen   68

Are rare, and so are they.

Troy.   Beare with him Ladies.

Mor. He is a foule-mouth'd man.

Sec. [Aside to Mor.] Whore, bitch ----

Fox, treedle ---- fa la la la ----

Mor. How's that my Cat a Mountaine?

Spa.   Hold her there Boy.

Cla. Were you ere in love, fine Signior?

Rom.   Yes for sports sake;   74

But soone forgot it. He that rides a gallop

Is quickly weary. I esteem of Love

As of a man in some huge place; it puzzles

Reason, distracts the freedome of the soule;

Renders a wise man foole, and a foole wise

In's owne conceit, not else. It yeelds effects   80

42 Of pleasure, travaile; bitter, sweet; warre,

peace;   81

Thornes, roses; prayers, curses; longings,

surfets;

Despaire, and then a rope. Oh my trim lover,   83

Yes, I have loved a score at once.

    <u>Spa</u>. Out stallion, as I am a man and no

man, the Baboon lies, I dare sweare, abominably.   86

    <u>Sec</u>. Inhumanly! ---- [Pinches Mor.] Keepe

your bow close, <u>vixen</u>.   88

    <u>Mor</u>. [Aside to Sec.] Beshrew your fingers

    If you be in earnest.   89

You pinch too hard. Go to, Ile pare your nailes

    for't.   90

    <u>Spa</u>. [Aside to Sec.] She meanes your

hornes. There's a bob for you.   92

    <u>Cla</u>. Spruice Signior, if a man may love

    so many,

Why may not a faire Lady have like priviledge

Of several servants?

    <u>Troy</u>.   Answer that! The reason   95

Holds the same weight.

    <u>Mor</u>.   Marry and so it does,

Tho he would spit his gall out.

    <u>Spa</u>. [Aside to Sec.]   Marke that <u>Secco</u>.

    <u>Sil</u>. De'e pumpe for a reply?

    <u>Rom</u>.   The learned differ

In that point; grand and famous Schollers often

Have argued <u>pro</u> and <u>con</u>, and left it doubtfull;

Volumes have been writ on't. If then great

    Clerkes

Suspend their resolutions, 'tis a modestie

For me to silence mine.

<u>Flo</u>.   Dull and phlegmatick.

<u>Cla</u>. Yet women sure in such a case are ever

More secret then men are.

<u>Sil</u>.   Yea and talke lesse.

<u>Rom</u>. That is a truth much fabled, never

found.   106

You secret? when your Dresses blab your vani-

ties: 107

<u>Carnation</u> for your Points? there's a grosse

babler;   108

<u>Tawny</u>? hey ho, the pretty heart is wounded; 109

A knot of <u>Willow</u> Ribbands? she's forsaken; 110

Another rides the Cock-horse, <u>green</u> <u>and</u> <u>azure</u>

Wince and cry wee hee like a Colt unbroken;   112

43 But desperate <u>black</u> puts 'em in minde of fish

daies;   113

When Lent spurres on Devotion, there's a famine. 114

Yet love and judgement may helpe all this pudder.

Where are they? Not in females!

<u>Flo</u>.   In all sorts of men no doubt.   116

<u>Sil</u>. Else they were sots to choose.

<u>Cla</u>. To sweare and flatter, sometimes

ly for profit.

    <u>Rom</u>. Not so forsooth. Should love and

    judgement meet,   119

The old, the foole, the ugly and deform'd   120

Could never be beloved; for example,

Behold these two- this Madam and this shaver. 122

    <u>Mor</u>. I doe defie thee! Am I old or ugly? 123

    <u>Sec</u>. Tricks, knacks, devices. Now it

troules about.   125

    <u>Rom</u>. Troule let it stripling. Thou hast

    yet firme footing,   126

And needst not feare the Cuckolds livory.

There's good Philosophie for't. Take this for

    comfort: 128

No horned Beasts have teeth in either gummes; 129

But thou art tooth'd on both sides, tho she

    faile in't.

    <u>Mor</u>. He's not jealous Sirrah.

    <u>Rom</u>.   That's his Fortune. 131

Women indeed more jealous are then Men;

But men have more cause.

    <u>Spa</u>. There a' rub'd your forehead. 'Twas

a tough blow.   135

    <u>Sec</u>. It smarts.

    <u>Mor</u>. Pox on him! Let him   137

Put's finger into any Gums of mine.   138

He shall finde <u>I</u> have teeth about me, sound

    ones.

    <u>Sec</u>. You are a scurvie fellow, and I am

made a Cokes, an Asse; and this same filthy

Cron's a flirt. <u>Whope do me no harme good Wo-

man</u>.

                         Exit Secco.   03

    <u>Spa</u>. [Aside] Now now he's in, <u>I</u> must not

leave him so.

                      Exit Spadone.   04

    <u>Troy</u>. <u>Morosa</u>, what meanes this?

    <u>Mor</u>.   I know not, <u>I</u>.   146

He pinched me, called me names, most filthy

    names.

[To Rom.] Will ye part hence Sir? <u>I</u> will set

    ye packing.   148

                      Exit Morosa.   05

    <u>Cla</u>. You were indeed too broad, too violent.

44   <u>Flo</u>. Here's nothing meant but mirth.

    <u>Sil</u>.   The Gentleman

Hath been a little pleasant.

    <u>Cla</u>.   Somewhat bitter

Against our sex.

    <u>Cas</u>.   For which I promise him

A' ne're proves choise of mine.

<u>Rom</u>.   Not I your choice.   153

<u>Troy</u>. So she protested Signior.

<u>Rom</u>.   Indeed.

                    Enter Morosa.   06

<u>Cla</u>. Why, you are mov'd Sir?

<u>Mor</u>.   Hence, there enters   155
A civiller companion for faire Ladies
Then such a sloven.

    <u>Rom</u>.   Beauties.

    <u>Troy</u>.   Time prevents us.   157
Love and sweet thoughts accompany this presence.

                    Exit Troylo and Romanello.   07

Enter Octavio, Secco whispering him, Livio and
    Nitido.

    <u>Oct</u>. Enough, slip off, and on your life
    be secret.

                              Exit Secco.
A lovely day, young creatures. To you <u>Floria</u>;
To you <u>Clarella</u>, <u>Silvia</u>, to all service.   161

But who is this faire stranger?

    <u>Liv.</u>   <u>Castamela</u>,
My Sister, noble Lord.

    <u>Oct.</u>   Let ignorance
Of what you were, plead my neglect of manners,
And this soft touch excuse it. Y'ave inriched   165
This little family (most excellent Virgin)
With th' honour of your company.

    <u>Cas.</u>   I finde them
Worthily gracefull Sir.

    <u>Liv.</u> [Aside]   Are ye so taken?

    <u>Oct.</u> Here are no publique sights nor Court-
    ly visitants,
Which youth and active blood might stray in
    thought for.   170
The companies are few, the pleasures single,
And rarely to be brook'd, perhaps by any   172
Not perfectly acquainted with this custome.   173
Are they not lovely one?

    <u>Liv.</u>   Sir, I dare answer
My sisters resolution. Free converse
Amongst so many of her Sex, so vertuous,
She ever hath prefer'd before the surquedry
Of protestation, or the vainer giddinesse
Of popular attendants.

45

Musicke.

Cas. [Aside]   Well playd Brother.

Oct. The meaning of this Musicke?

Mor.   Please your Lordship,   180
It is the Ladies hower for exercise
In Song and Dance.

Oct.   I dare not be the Author
Of trewanting the time then, neither will I.

Mor. Walke on deere Ladies.

Oct.   'Tis a taske of pleasure.

Liv. [Aside to Castamela] Be now my Sister;
stand a triall bravely.   185

Mor. [Aside to Castamela] Remember my instruc-
tions, or ----

                Exit all but Octavio and Castamela. 011

Oct.   With pardon.
You are not of the number I presume yet,
To be enjoyn'd to houres. If you please,
We for a little while may sit as Judges
Of their proficience. Pray vouchsafe the favour. 190

Cas. I am Sir in a place to be commanded,
As now the present urgeth.

Oct.   No compulsion,
That were too hard a word; where you are Soveraigne

Your yea and nay is Law. I have a suit t'ee.   194

    <u>Cas</u>. For what Sir?

    <u>Oct</u>.   For your love.

    <u>Cas</u>.   To whom? I am not
So weary of th' authority I hold

46 Over mine owne contents in sleepes and wakings   197
That Ide resigne my liberty to any
Who should controule it.

    <u>Oct</u>.   Neither <u>I</u> intend so.   199
Grant me an entertainment.

    <u>Cas</u>.   Of what nature?

    <u>Oct</u>. To aknowledge me your creature.

    <u>Cas</u>.   Oh my Lord.
You are too wise in yeeres, too full of coun-
    saile
For my greene inexperience.

    <u>Oct</u>.   Love <u>deare Maid</u>,
Is but desire of beauty, and 'tis proper
For beauty to desire to be belov'd.
<u>I</u> am not free from passion. Tho the current   206
Of a more lively heate runnes slowly through me,
My heart is gentle, and beleeve <u>fresh Girle</u>,   208
Thou shalt not wish for any full addition,
Which may adorne thy rarities to boast 'em,   210
That bounty can withhold. This <u>Academy</u>   211

Of silent pleasures is maintain'd, but onely

To such a constant use.

     Cas.   You have belike then

A Patent for concealing Virgins; otherwise   214

Make plainer your intentions.

     Oct.   To be pleasant

In practise of some outward sences onely-   216

No more.

     Cas.   No worse you dare not to imagine,   217

Where such an awfull Innocencie, as mine is,

Out-faces every wickednesse your dotage   219

Has lul'd you in. I scent your cruell mercies.   220

Your factresse hath been tampering for my

     misery.   221

Your old temptation; your shee-Devill ---- Beare

     with   222

A language which this place, and none but this,

     hath

Infected my tongue with. The time will come

     too,

When he (unhappy man) whom your advancement

47 Hath ruin'd by being Spannell to your fortunes,

Will curse a' train'd me hither. ---- Livio,   227

I must not call him Brother; this one act

Hath rent him off the ancestry he sprung from.

<u>Oct</u>. The proffer of a noble courtesie
Is checkt it seemes.

    <u>Cas</u>.   A courtesie? a bondage!   231
You are a great man vicious, much more vic-
    ious,
Because you hold a seeming league with charity
Of pestilent nature, keeping hospitality
For sensualists in your owne Sepulchre,
Even by your life time; yet are dead already.   236

    <u>Oct</u>. How's this? Come be more mild.

    <u>Cas</u>.   You chide me soberly.   237
Then Sir <u>I</u> tune my voice to other Musique.   238
You are an eminent statist, be a Father
To such unfriended Virgins, as your bounty
Hath drawn into a scandall. You are power-
    full   241
In meanes, a Batchelour, freed from the jelous-
    ies   242
Of wants. Convert this privacie of maintenance   243
Into your own Court; let this (as you call it)   244
Your <u>Academy</u> have a residence there;
And there survey your charity your selfe:
That when you shall bestow on worthy husbands
With fitting portions, such as you know worthie,   248
You may yeeld to the present age example,

And to posterity a glorious Chronicle.   250

There were a worke of piety; the other is   251

A scorne upon your Tombe-stone, where the Reader   252

Will but expound, that when you liv'd you pan-

    der'd

Your owne purse and your fame. I am too bold

    Sir,

Some anger and some pittie hath directed

A wandring trouble.

    Oct.   Be not known what passages

The time hath lent, for once I can beare with yee.

    Cas. Ile countenance the hazzard of suspition.

48 And be your guest a while.

    Oct.   Be ---- but hereafter ----

I know not what. ---- Livio.

Enter Livio and Morosa.

    Liv.   My Lord.

    Cas.   Indeed Sir   260

I cannot part w'ee yet.

    Oct.   Well then thou shalt not,   261

My pretious Castamela ---- thou hast a Sister,

A perfect Sister Livio.

Mor. [Aside]   All is inck'd here. 263
Good soule indeed.

Liv. [Aside to Cast.] Ide speak with you anon.

Cas. [Aside to Liv.] It may be so.

Oct.   Come faire one.

Liv. [Aside]   Oh I am cheated.

                                All Exit. 013

                          Act IV

[IV. i]

                    Enter Livio and Castamela.

     Liv. Prithee be serious.

     Cas.   Prithee interupt not
The Paradise of my becharming thoughts,
Which mount my knowledge to the spheare I move
     in,
Above this uselesse tattle.

     Liv.   Tattle? Sister,
D'ee know to whom you talke this?

     Cas.   To the Gentleman   5
Of my Lords Horse, new stept into the Office.   6
'Tis a good place Sir, if you can be thankfull.
Demeane your carriage in it, so that negligence
Or pride of your preferment oversway not
The grace you hold in his esteem. Such fortunes
Drop not down every day; observe the favour
49 That rais'd you to this fortune.

     Liv.   Thou mistak'st sure
What person thou holdst speech with.

     Cas.   Strange and idle.

     Liv. Ist possible? Why? you are turn'd

        a Mistris,   14

A Mistris of the trimme; beshrew me Lady,   15

You keepe a stately Port, but it becomes you not.

Our Fathers Daughter, if I erre not rarely,

Delighted in a softer humbler sweetnes,   18

Not in a hey-de-gay of scurvey Gallantry.   19

You do not brave it like a thing o'th'fashion;   20

You ape the humor faintly.

        Cas.   Love deare Maid

Is but desire of beauty, and 'tis proper

For beauty to desire to be belov'd.

        Liv.   Fine sport.   23

You mind not me; will you yet heare me   24

        Madam?

        Cas. Thou shalt not wish for any full ad-

        dition,

Which may adorne thy rarities to boast 'em,   26

That bounty can withold. ---- I know I shall

        not.   27

        Liv. And so you clapt the bargaine; the con-

        ceit on't   28

Tickles your contemplation. 'Tis come out now;   29

A Womans tongue I see, some time or other

Will prove her Traytor. This was all I sifted,   31

And here have found thee wretched.

    <u>Cas</u>.   We shall flourish,   32

Feed high henceforth, man, and no more be streigh-

    tend

Within the limits of an emptie patience,   34

Nor tire our feeble eyes with gazing onely

On greatnes, which enjoyes the swindge of plea-

    sures.

But be our selves the object of their envie,

To whom a service would have seem'd ambition,

It was thy cunning <u>Livio</u>; <u>I</u> applaud it.   39

Feare nothing; Ile be thrifty in thy projects.   40

Want misery? may all such want as thinke on't;

Our footing shall stand firme.

50   <u>Liv</u>.   You are much witty.

Why <u>Castamela</u>, this to me? You counterfeit   43

Most palpablie. <u>I</u> am too well acquainted

With thy condition Sister; if the Marquesse

Hath utter'd one unchaste, one wanton syllable,

Provoking thy contempt, not all the flatteries   47

Of his assurance to our hopes of rising,

Can or shall slave our soules.

    <u>Cas</u>.   Indeed not so Sir.   49

You are beside the point, most <u>gentle</u> <u>Signior</u>.   50

Ile be no more your ward, no longer chamber'd,

Nor mew'd up to the lure of your Devotion.   52

Trust me.   I must not, will not, dare not;

    surely   53

I cannot.   For my promise past, and sufferance   54

Of former trialls hath too strongly arm'd me.   55

You may take this for answer.

    Liv.   In such earnest?

Hath goodnes left thee quite?   Foole thou art

    wandring   57

In dangerous fogges, which will corrupt the pur-

    itie

Of every noble vertue dwelt within thee.

Come home againe, home Castamela, Sister;   60

Home to thine owne simplicitie, and rather

Then yeeld thy memorie up to the Witch-craft

Of an abused confidence, be courted   63

For Romanello.

    Cas.   Romanello.

    Liv.   Scornst thou

The name?   Thy thoughts I finde then are chang'd

    rebells   65

To all that's honest, that's to truth and honour.

    Cas.   So Sir, and in good time.

    Liv.   Thou art falne suddainly

Into a plurisie of faithlesse impudence;

A whorish itch infects thy blood, a leprosie   69

Of raging lust, and thou art madde to prostitute

The glory of thy Virgin dower basely

For common sale. This foulenesse must be purg'd,

51 Or thy disease will ranckle to a pestilence,

Which can even taint the very ayre about thee.   74

But I shall studie Physick.

     Cas.   Learne good manners!   75

I take it you are sawcie.

     Liv.   Sawcie? strumpet

In thy desires. 'Tis in my power to cut off   77

The twist thy life is spunne by.

     Cas.   Phew, you rave now.   78

But if you have not perished all your reason,

Know I will use my freedome; you (forsooth)

For change of fresh apparell, and the pocketting

Of some well looking Duccats, were contented,

Passinglie pleas'd, yes marry were you (marke it)

To expose me to the danger now you raile at.

Brought me, nay forc'd me hither, without question

Of what might follow. Here you find the issue   86

And I distrust not but it was th' appointment

Of some succeeding fate that more concern'd me

Then widdowed virginity.

     Liv.   You are gallant,   89

One of my old Lord Fancies   Peevish girle,

Was't ever heard that youth could doate on sick-
     nesse,

A gray beard, wrinckled face, a dryed up marrow,

A toothlesse head, ---- a ---- this is but a
     merriment,

Meerely but triall. <u>Romanello</u> loves thee,

Has not abundance, true, yet cannot want.

Returne with me, and <u>I</u> will leave these fortunes,

Good Maid, of gentle nature.

    <u>Cas</u>.   By my hopes,

<u>I</u> never plac'd affection on that Gentleman,

Tho a' deserv'd well; <u>I</u> have told him often   99

My resolution.

    <u>Liv</u>.   Will you hence, and trust to

My care of setling you a peace.

    <u>Cas</u>.   No surely,

52 Such treatie may breake off.

    <u>Liv</u>.   Off bee't broken!   102

Ile doe what thou shalt rue.

    <u>Cas</u>.   You cannot <u>Livio</u>.

    <u>Liv</u>. So confident? Young Mistris mine,

    Ile do't.   104

                      Exit Livio.   02

Enter Troylo.

Troy. Incomparable Maid.

Cas.   You have been Counsellor

To a strange Dialogue.

Troy.   If there be constancie

In protestation of a vertuous nature,   107

You are secure, as the effects shall witnes.

Cas. Be noble- I am credulous   my lan-

guage   109

Hath prejudic'd my heart; I and my Brother

Ne're parted at such distance; yet I glory   111

In the faire race he runs. But feare the

violence   112

Of his disorder.

Troy.   Little time shall quit him.

Enter Secco leading Nitido in a Garter with one

hand, a Rod in his other; followed by

Morosa, Silvia, Floria, Clarella;

Spadone behind laughing.

Sec. The young Whelp is mad. I must slice   114

the worme out of his breech. I have noos'd his   115

neck in the Collar; and I will once turne Dogleech. Stand from about me, or you'l finde me
terrible and furious.

    Nit. Ladies, good Ladies, deare Madam   119
Morosa.

    Flo. Honest Secco.

    Sil. What was the cause? What wrong has   122
hee done to thee?

    Cla. Why dost thou fright us so, and art
so peremptory where wee are present fellow?

    Mor. Honey-bird, Spouse, Catamountaine;
ah the Child, the pretty poore Child; the sweet
fac'd Child.

    Spa. That very word halters the eare-wig.

    Sec. Off I say, or I shall lay bare all the
naked truth to your faces. His foreparts have   131
been so lusty, and his posterions must do pen-
ance for't. Untrusse Whiskin, untrusse; away   133
burres, out Mare-hagge moyle- avaunt, thy   134
turne comes next. The Horns of my rage are ad-   135
vanced! Hence or I shall gore ye.   136

    Spa. Lash him soundly. Let the little   137
Ape shew trickes.

    Nit. Helpe, or I shall be throtled.

    Mor. Yes, I will helpe thee pretty heart.   140

53

If my tongue cannot prevaile; my nayles shall.

Barbarous minded man, let go, or I shall use my

tallons.

    Spa. Well playd Dog, well playd Beare!   144

Fa, fa, fa! To't, to't.   145

    Sec. Fury, whore, baud, my Wife and the

Devill.

    Mor. Tospot, stinckard, pander, my husband

and a rascal.   149

    Spa. Scould, Coxcombe, baggage, Cuckold.   150

        Cràbed Age and Youth

        Cannot jumpe together:

        One is like good lucke,

        T' other like foule weather.

    Troy. Let us fall in now. What uncivill

rudenesse   155

Dares offer a disturbance to this company.

Peace and delights dwell here, not brawles and

    outrage.   157

Sirrah be sure you shew some reasons why

You so forget your duty? Quickly shew it,   159

Or I shall tame your choller. What's the

    ground on't?   160

    Spa. Humh, how's that? How's that? Is   161

he there with a Wanion? Then doe I begin to

dwindle. ---- O oh, the fit, the fit; the fits   163
upon me now, now now now.

  Sec. It shall out. First then know all
Christian people, Jewes and Infidels, hees and   166
shees, by these presents, that I am a beast;
see what I say, I say a very beast.

  Troy. 'Tis granted.

  Sec. Go to then, a horned beast, a goodly   170
tall horn'd beast, in pure verity a Cuckold.   171
Nay I will tickle their Trangdidoes.

  Mor. Ah thou base fellow! wouldst thou
confesse it and it were so. But 'tis not so,   174
and thou lyest and lowdly.

  Troy. Patience Morosa. You are you say
a Cuckold.   176

54 Sec. Ile justifie my words; I scorn to
eate 'em. This sucking Ferret hath been wrig-   178
ling in my old Coney borough.

  Mor. The Boy, the Babe, the Infant! I   180
spit at thee.

  Cas. Fie Secco fie.

  Sec. Appeare Spadone. My proofes are preg-   183
nant and grosse. Truth is the truth; I must and   184
I will be divorced. Speake Spadone and exalt   185
thy voice.

    <u>Spa</u>. Who <u>I</u> speake? Alas <u>I</u> cannot speake,   187
<u>I</u>.

    <u>Nit</u>. As <u>I</u> hope to live to be a man.

    <u>Sec</u>. Damne the prick of thy weason Pipe.   190
Where but two lie in a bed you must be Bodkin
bitch-baby, must ye. <u>Spadone</u>, am <u>I</u> a Cuckold   192
or no Cuckold?

    <u>Spa</u>. Why? you know <u>I</u> am an ignorant unable   194
trifle in such businesse; an Oafe, a simple
Alcatote; an Innocent.

    <u>Sec</u>. Nay nay nay, no matter for that; this
Ramkin hath tup'd my old rotten carrion Mutton.

    <u>Mor</u>. Rotten in thy maw, thy guts and
garbage.

    <u>Sec</u>. <u>Spadone</u> speake alowd what <u>I</u> am.

    <u>Spa</u>. <u>I</u> do not know.

    <u>Sec</u>. What has thou seen 'em doing to-   203
gether? Doing.   204

    <u>Spa</u>. Nothing

    <u>Mor</u>. Are thy mad braines in thy mazar
now, thou jealous Bedlam?

    <u>Sec</u>. Didst not thou from time to time tell
me as much?

    <u>Spa</u>. Never.

    <u>Sec</u>. Heyday, Ladies and Signior <u>I</u> am a-
bus'd. They are agreed to scorne, jeere and runne   212

me out of my wits; by consent this gelded hobet

a hoy is a corrupted Pander; the page a milke   214

livered Dildo; my Wife a Whore confest; and I my

selfe a Cuckold arrant.

    Spa. Truely <u>Secco</u>, for the antient good   217

Woman, I dare sweare point-blanck; and the Boy   218

surely, I ever said was to any mans thinking, a

very Chrisome in the thing you wot. That's my   220

opinion clearely.

    <u>Cla</u>. What a wise goose-cap hast thou

shew'd thy self?

    <u>Sec</u>. Here in my fore-head it sticks, and

55 stick it shall. Law I will have; I will never   224

more tumble in sheets with thee; I will father

no mis-begotten of thine; the Court shall

trounce thee, the Citie casheere thee, diseases

devoure thee, and the Spittle confound thee.

                            Exit Secco.   04

    <u>Cas</u>. The man has dream'd himselfe into a

lunacie.   229

    <u>Sil</u>. Alas poore <u>Nitido</u>.

    <u>Nit</u>.   Truely I am innocent.

    <u>Mor</u>. Marry art thou, so thou art. The   231

World sayes how vertuously I have carried my good

name in every part about me, these threescore

yeares and odde; and at last to slip with a

child! There are men, men enough, tough and   235

lustie (I hope) if one would give their mind to

the iniquitie of the flesh, but this is the life

I ha' led with him a while since when a' lies by   238

me as cold as a dry stone.

    Troy. This onely (Ladies) is a fit of

    noveltie.   240

All will be reconcil'd. I doubt, Spadone,   241

Here is your hand in this how e're deny'd.   242

    Spa. Faithfully in truth forsooth.

    Troy. Well, well enough ---- Morosa.

    be lesse troubled;

This little jarre is argument of love.   245

It will prove lasting; beauties, I attend yee.

           Exit all but Spadone and Nitido.   05

    Spa. Youngling, a word youngling. Have   247

not you scap'd the lash hansomly? Thanke me for't. 248

    Nit. I feare thy roguery, and I shall finde

it.

    Spa. Ist possible! Give me thy little   251

fist. We are friends; have a care henceforth;   252

remember this whilst you live. And still the

Urchin would, but could not doe: Pretty knave,

and so forth. Come, truce on all hands.   255

<u>Nit</u>. Beshrew your fooles head; this was
jeast in earnest.

                              Exit Spadone and Nitido.   06
[IV. ii]

                    Enter Romanello.

<u>Rom</u>. I will converse with beasts; there
        is in mankinde
No sound society, but in woman (blesse me)
Nor faith nor reason: I may justly wonder
What trust was in my Mother.

                    Enter a Servant.

56   <u>Ser</u>.   A Caroch, sir,
Stands at the Gate.

        <u>Rom</u>.   Stand let it still, and freeze there.   5
Make sure the locks.

        <u>Ser</u>.   Too late. You are prevented.   6

        Enter Flavia, Camillo, and Vespuci.

<u>Fla</u>. Brother, I come ----

<u>Rom</u>.   Unlookt for;----I but sojourne

My selfe; I keepe nor house, nor entertain-

    ments.   8

French Cookes compos'd, Italian Collations   9

Rich Persian surfets, with a traine of services,

Befitting exquisite Ladies, such as you are,

Perfume not our low Roofes; - the way lies open.   12

That there: ---- Good day, great Madam.

    <u>Fla</u>.   Why d'yee slight me?

For what one act of mine, even from my Child-

    hood,

Which may deliver my deserts inferiour

Or to our Births or Familie, is Nature   16

Become, in your contempt of me, a Monster?

    <u>Ves</u>. [Aside to Cam.] What's this <u>Camillo</u>!

    <u>Cam</u>. [Aside to Ves.]   Not the straine in

    ordinary.

    <u>Rom</u>. I'm out of tune to chop discourses; ---

    however,   19

You are a Woman.

    <u>Fla</u>.   Pensive and unfortunate,

Wanting a Brothers boscme to dis-burthen

More griefs, then female weaknesse can keep

    league with.   22

Let worst of malice, voyc'd in loud report,

Spit what it dares invent against my actions;

And it shall never find a power to blemish

My mention, other then beseemes a patient.   26

I repine not at lownesse; and the Fortunes   27

Which I attend on now, are as I value them,

No new creation to a looser liberty.   29

Your strangenes only may beget a change

In wild opinion.

57   Cam. [Aside to Ves.] Heere's another tang of sence,

Vespuci.   31

        Ves. [Aside to Cam.]   Listen and observe.   32

        Rom. Are not you pray ye- (nay, wee'l be

        contented   33

In presence of your Ushers, once to prattle

Some idle minutes)- are you not inthroan'd   35

The Ladie Regent, by whose speciall influence

Julio the Count of Camerine is order'd?

        Fla. His Wife 'tis knowne I am; and in that

        title,

Obedient to a service: else, of greatnesse

The quiet of my wish was ne're ambitious.   40

        Rom. Hee loves you?

        Fla.   As worthily, as dearely.

        Rom. And 'tis beleev'd how practice

        quickly fashion'd

A port of humorous acticknesse in carriage,

Discourse, demeanour, gestures.

    <u>Cam</u>. [Aside]   Put home roundly.

    <u>Ves</u>. [Aside] A ward for that blow.

    <u>Fla</u>.   Safety, of mine Honor,

Instructed such deceit.

    Rom.   Your honour?

    <u>Fla</u>.   Witnesse

This brace of sprightly Gallants, whose confed-

    eracie

Presum'd to plot a siege.

    <u>Cam</u>. <u>Ves</u>.   Wee, Madam!

    <u>Rom</u>.   On, on,

Some leysure serves us now.

    <u>Fla</u>.   Still as Lord <u>Julio</u>

Pursu'd his Contract with the man (oh pardon

If I forget to name him) by whose poverty

Of honest truth, I was renounc'd in Marriage,   52

These two, intrusted for a secret Courtship,

By tokens, letters, message, in their turnes

Proffered their owne devotions, as they term'd

    them,

Almost unto an impudence; regardlesse

Of him, on whose supportance they relyed.

      <u>Rom</u>. Dare not for both your lives to in-

      terrupt her.

58   Fla. Bayted thus to vexation, I assum'd
        A dulnesse of simplicity; till afterwards,   60
        Lost to my Citie, Freedome, and now enter'd
        Into this present state of my Condition,   62
        (Concluding henceforth absolute security
        From their lascivious Villanies) I continued
        My former custome of ridiculous lightnesse,
        As they did their pursuit. T' acquaint my Lord,
            were   66
        T' have ruin'd their best certainty of living.   67
        But that might yeeld suspition in my nature;
        And woman may be vertuous without mischiefe,
        To such as tempt them.

            Rom.   You are much to blame sirs,
        Should all be truth is utterd.

            Fla.   For that Justice
        I did command them hither, for a privacie
        In conference 'twixt Flavia and her brother
        Needed no Secretaries such as these are.   74
        Now Romanello, thou art every refuge
        I flie for right to; if I be thy Sister,
        And not a Bastard, answer their confession,
        Or threaten vengeance, with perpetuall silence.

            Cam. My follies are acknowledg'd; y'are a
            Lady

Who have outdone example. When I trespasse   80

In ought but duty, and respects of service,

May hopes of joyes forsake me.

    <u>Ves</u>.   To like pennance

I joyne a constant votarie.

    <u>Rom</u>.   Peace then

Is ratified.--My Sister thou hast waken'd   84

Intranc'd affection from its sleepe to knowledge

Of once more who thou art; no jealous frenzie

Shall hazard a distrust. Reigne in thy sweetnes,   87

Thou onely worthy Woman; these two Converts

Record our hearty union. I have shooke off   89

My thraldome Lady, and have made discoveries

59 Of famous Novels; but of those hereafter;

Thus wee seale love. [Takes her hand] You

    shall know all and wonder.   92

Enter Livio

    <u>Liv</u>. Health and his hearts desire to <u>Rom-</u>

    <u>anello</u>;

My welcome I bring with me. Noblest Lady,   94

Excuse an ignorance of your faire presence;

This may be bold intrusion.

Fla.   Not by me, Sir.

Rom. You are not frequent here as I remember;

But since you bring your welcome with you, Livio,

Be bold to use it- to the point.

Liv.   This Lady,   99

With both these Gentlemen, in happie houre

May be partakers of the long liv'd amity,

Our soules must linke in.

Rom.   So belike the Marquesse   102

Stores some new grace, some speciall close employment,

For whom your kind commends, by deputation,   104

Please thinke on to oblige, and Livio's charity

Descends on Romanello liberally,   106

Above my means to thank.

Liv.   Siena sometimes

Has beene inform'd how gladly there did passe

A treatie of chast loves with Castamela;

From this good heart, it was in me an error

Wilfull and causelesse, 'tis confest, that
hinder'd

Such honourable prosecution,

Even and equall; better thoughts consider   113

How much I wrong'd the gentle course which led

yee

To vowes of true affection, us of friendship.   115

   Rom. Sits the wind there boy; leaving

   formall circumstance,   116

Proceed; you dally yet.

   Liv.   Then without plea,

For countenancing what has beene injurious

On my part, I am come to tender really

My Sister a lov'd Wife t'yee; freely take her

Right honest man, and as yee live together,

60 May your encrease of yeares prove but one spring,

One lasting flourishing youth. She is your owne.   123

My hands shall perfect what's requir'd to cere-

   mony.

   Fla. Brother, this day was meant a holy-

   day,

For feast on every side.

   Rom.   The new-turn'd Courtier

Proffers most franckly; but withall leaves out

A due consideration of the narrownesse

Our short estate is bounded in. Some Politicks   129

As they rise up (like Livio) to perfection

In their owne competencies, gather also

Grave supplement of providence and wisedome;

Yet he abates in his. ---- You use a triumph   133

In your advantages. It smels of state.   134

We know you are no foole.

    <u>Fla.</u>   Sooth I beleeve him.

    <u>Cam.</u> Else 'twere imposture.

    <u>Ves.</u>   Folly ranck, and sence lesse.

    <u>Liv.</u> Enjoyne an oath at large.

    <u>Rom.</u>   Since you meane earnest,

Receive in satisfaction; I am resolv'd

For single life; there was a time (was <u>Livio</u>)

When indiscretion blinded forecast in me;

But recollection, with your rules of thriftinesse,

Prevaild against all passion.

    <u>Liv.</u>   You'd be courted.   142

Courtship's the childe of coynesse <u>Romanello</u>;

And for the Rules 'tis possible to name them.

    <u>Rom.</u> A single life's no burthen; but to

    draw

In yoakes is chargeable, and doth require

A double maintenance. <u>Livio's</u> very words,   147

For he can live without a wife and purchase.   148

By'r Lady so you doe Sir. Send you joy on't.   149

These rules you see are possible, and answer'd.

    <u>Liv.</u> Full ---- answer was late made to this

    already.   151

My Sister's onely thine.

61   <u>Rom</u>.   Where lives the Creature

Your pitty stoopes to pin upon your servant?

Not in a Nunn'ry for a yeares probation?

Fie on such coldnes. There are Bowres Of Fancies   155

Ravish'd from troops of Fairy Nymphs, and Virgins

Cul'd from the downie breasts of Queenes their

        Mothers,

In the <u>Titanian</u> Empire, far from Mortals:

But these are tales. Troth I have quite abandoned   159

All loving humour.

        <u>Liv</u>.   Heere is scorne in Riddles.   160

        <u>Rom</u>. Were there another Marquesse in <u>Sienna</u>

More potent than the same who is vice-gerent

To the great Duke of <u>Florence</u>, our grand Master;   163

Were the <u>great</u> <u>Duke</u> himselfe here, and would

        lift up

My head to fellow pompe amongst his Nobles,

By falshood to the honour of <u>a</u> <u>Sister</u>,

Urging me instrument in his <u>Seraglio</u>;

Ide teare the Wardrobe of an outside from him

Rather than live a Pandar to his bribery.

        <u>Liv</u>. So would the <u>hee</u> you talke to, <u>Rom</u>-

        <u>anello</u>,

Without a noise that's singular.

        <u>Rom</u>.   Shee's Countesse   171

<u>Flavia</u>, shee; but she has an Earle her Husband,

Though farre from our procurement.

    <u>Liv</u>.   Castamela

Is refus'd then.

    <u>Rom</u>.   Never design'd my Choyce.   174

You know and I know (<u>Livio</u>), more I tell thee,   175

A noble honestie ought to give allowance,

When reason intercedes; by all that's manly,

I range not in derision, but compassion.

    <u>Liv</u>. Intelligence flies swiftly.

    <u>Rom</u>.   Pretty swiftly.   179

We have compar'd the Copie with th' <u>Originall</u>,

And finde no disagreement.

    <u>Liv</u>.   So my Sister

62 Can be no wife for <u>Romanello</u>?

    <u>Rom</u>.   No, no,

One noe, once more and ever. ---- This your cour-

tesie   183

Foild me a second. ---- Sir, you brought a wel-

come,   184

You must not part without it. Scan with pittie   185

My plainnesse; I intend nor gall, nor quarrell.   186

    <u>Liv</u>. Far bee't from me to presse a blame,

    great Lady;

I kisse your noble hands, and to these Gentlemen

Present a civill parting. Romanello,   189

By the next foot-Post thou wilt heare some newes

Of alteration; if I send, come to me.

    Rom. Questionlesse, yea.

    Liv.   My thanks may quit the favor.

                          Exit Livio. 05

    Fla. Brother his intercourse of conference,

Appeares at once perplext, but withall sensible.

    Rom. Doubts easily resolv'd. Upon your

vertues   195

The whole foundation of my peace is grounded.   196

Ile guard yee to your home. Lost in one com-

fort   197

Heere I have found another.

    Fla.   Goodnesse prosper it.

              Exit Romanello and Flavia.   06

Act V

[V. i]

Enter Octavio, Troylo, Secco, and Nitido.

Oct. No more of these complaints and clam-
ors;
Have we nor enemies abroad, nor waking Syco-
phants,   2
Who peering through our actions, wait occasion
By which they watch to lay advantage open
To vulgar descant, but amongst our selves
Some whom we call our owne must practise scandall
(Out of a libertie of ease and fulnesse)
Against our honour. We shall quickly order   8
Strange reformation Sirs, and you will find it.
63   Troy. When Servants servants, slaves, once
relish license
Of good opinion from a noble nature,
They take upon them boldnesse to abuse
Such interest, and Lord it o're their fellowes,   13
As if they were exempt from that condition.
Oct. He is unfit to mannage publique matters
Who knowes not how to rule at home his house-
hold.   16

You must be jealous (puppie) of a Boy too;

Raise uprores, bandie noise amongst young Maidens;   18

Keepe revels in your madnesse; use authoritie   19

Of giving punishment. A foole must foole ye;   20

And this is all but pastime, as you thinke it.

    Nit. With your good Lordships favor. Since,

    Spadone   22

Confest it was a gullery put on Secco,

For some revenge meant me.

    Troy.   He vow'd it truth

Before the Ladies in my hearing.

    Oct.   Sirrah,

Ile turne you to your shop agen and trinkets,

Your sudes and pan of small-cole. Take your dam-

    zell   27

The grand old ragg, of beautie, your deaths

    head;   28

Try then what custome reverence can trade in;

Fiddle, and play your pranks amongst your neigh-

    bours,   30

That all the towne may roare ye. Now ye simper   31

And looke like a shav'd skull.

    Nit.   This comes of prating.

    Sec. I am my Lord a worme. Pray my Lord

    tread on   33

Me, I will not turne agen; 'las I shall never

    venture   34

To hang my Pole out. On my knees I begge it,   35

My bare knees. I will downe unto my wife   36

And doe what she will have me, all I can doe;

Nay more, (if she will have it) aske forgivenes.   38

Be an obedient Husband; never crosse her.   39

Unlesse sometimes in kindnes. Seignior <u>Troylo</u>,   40

Speake one sweet word. Ile sweare 'twas in my

    madnes.

I said I knew not what, and that no creature

64 Was brought by you amongst the Ladies. <u>Nitido</u>   43

Ile forsweare thee too.

    <u>Oct</u>.   Wait a while our pleasure;

You shall know more anon.

      <u>Sec</u>.   Remember me now.

                  Exit Secco and Nitido.   02

    <u>Oct</u>. <u>Troylo</u>, thou art my brothers sonne,

    and neerest.

In blood to me; thou hast beene next in coun-

    sells.

Those ties of nature (if thou canst consider

How much they doe engage) worke by instinct

In every worthy or ignoble mention

Which can concerne me.

Troy.   Sir, they have and shall
As long as I beare life.

Oct.   Henceforth the Stewardship
My carefulnes, for the honour of our <u>Familie</u>,   53
Has undertooke, must yeeld the world account,
And make cleare reckonings; yet we stand
    suspected
In our even courses.

Troy.   But when time shall wonder
How much it was mistaken in the issue
Of honourable, and secure contrivements,   58
Your wisedome crown'd with lawrels of a Justice
Deserving approbation will quite foyle
The ignorance of popular opinion.

Oct. Report is merry with my feates;
    my dotage
Undoubtedly the Vulgar voyce doth caroll it.

Troy. True Sir, but <u>Romanello's</u> late
    admission
Warrants that giddy confidence of rumor
Without all contradiction; now'tis Oracle,
And so receiv'd. I am confirm'd, the Lady   67
By this time proves his scorne as well as
    laughter.

Oct. And we with her his table-talke. ----

                She stands not   69
        In any firme affection to him?

                Troy.   None Sir,   70
        More than her wonted Noblenesse afforded
        Out of a civill custome.

65   Oct.   We are resolute
        In our determination, meaning quickly
        To cause these clouds flie off; the ordering of it
        Nephew is thine.

                        Enter Livio.

                Troy.   Your care and love commands me
                Liv.   I come, my Lord, a Suiter.
                Oct.   Honest Livio,
        Perfectly honest, reallie; no fallacies
        No flawes are in thy truth.   I shall promote
                thee   78
        To place more eminent.
                Troy.   Livio deserves it.
                Oct.   What suit?   speake boldly.
                Liv.   Pray discharge my office,
        My mastership; 'twere better live a yeoman
        And live with men, then over-eye your houses,

Whiles I my selfe am ridden like a jade.

    <u>Oct</u>. Such breath sounds but ill manners.

    Know young man,   84

Old as we are, our Soule retaines a fire

Active and quick in motion, which shall equall

The daringst boyes ambition of true manhood

That weares a pride to brave us.

    <u>Troy</u>.   He is my friend, Sir.

    <u>Oct</u>. You are wearie of our service, and

    may leave it.

We can court no mans dutie.

    <u>Liv</u>.   Without passion,

My Lord, d'yee thinke your Nephew here, your

    <u>Troylo</u>

Parts in your spirit as freely as your blood?   92

'Tis no rude question.

    <u>Oct</u>.   Had you knowne his Mother

You might have sworne her honest; let him.

    justifie

Himselfe not base borne. For thy Sisters sake   95

I doe conceive the like of thee; be wiser,

But prate to me no more thus. -- If the gallant   97

Resolve on my attendance, ere he leave me,

Acquaint him with the present service, Nephew,

66 I meant to imploy him in.

                              Exit Octavio   04

     Troy.   Fie Livio! Wherefore   100
Turn'd wild upon the sodaine.

     Liv.   Pretty Gentleman,
How modestly you move your doubts? how tamely?
Aske Romanello. He hath without leave   103
Surveigh'd your Bowres of Fancies, hath dis-
     covered
The mystery of those pure Nuns; those chast ones,
Untouch'd forsooth; the holy Academie.   106
Hath found a Mothers daughter there of mine too,
And one who cald my Father Father. Talkes on't,   108
Ruffles in mirth on't; baffel'd to my face
The glory of her greatnesse by it.

     Troy.   Truely.

     Liv. Death to my sufferance! Canst thou
     heare this misery,   111
And answer't with a truely? 'Twas thy wickednes   112
False as thine owne heart tempted my credulity,
That her to ruine; she was once an innocent,   114
As free from spot, as the blew face of heaven
Without a cloud in't; she is now as sully'd
As is that Canopie, when mists and vapours
Divide it from our sight, and threaten pestilence.

     Troy. Sayes he so, Livio?

    <u>Liv.</u>   Yes, and't like your noblenes;   119
He truely does so say. Your breach of friend-
    ship   120
With me, must borrow courage from your Uncle,
Whiles your sword talkes an answer; there's
    no remedy;   122
I will have satisfaction, though thy life
Come short of such demand.
    <u>Troy.</u>   Then satisfaction
Much worthier then your sword can force, you
    shall have,
Yet mine shall keepe the peace; I can be angry
And brave alow'd in my reply; but honour
Schooles me to fitter grounds. This as a gentle-
    man   128
I promise, ere the minutes of the night   129
Warne us to rest, such satisfaction (heare me
67 And credit it) as more you cannot wish for,
So much not thinke of.
    <u>Liv.</u>   Not? The time is short.   132
Before our sleeping houre, you vow?
    <u>Troy.</u>   I doe,   133
Before we ought to sleepe.
    <u>Liv.</u>   So I intend to.   134
On confidence of which, what left the <u>Marquesse</u>

In charge for me? Ile do't.

    <u>Troy</u>.   Invite Count <u>Julio</u>,   136
His Ladie, and her brother, with their company
To my Lords Court at Supper.

    <u>Liv</u>.   Easie busines. 138
And then. ----

    <u>Troy</u>.   And then soone after, the performance
Of my past vow waites on yee, but be certaine
You bring them with ye.

    <u>Liv</u>.   Yet your servant.   141

    <u>Troy</u>. Neerer my friend, you'l find no lesse.

    <u>Liv</u>. 'Tis strange. Is't possible?   143

                Exit Troylo and Livio   05
[V. ii]
Enter Castamela, Clarella, Floria, and Silvia.

    <u>Cas</u>. You have discourst to me a lovely story;   1
My heart doth dance to th' musique; 'twere a
      sinne   2
Should I in any tittle stand distrustfull
Where such a people such as you are, innocent
Even by the Patent of your yeares and language,
Informe a truth. O talke it o're againe;   6
Ye are ye say <u>three</u> <u>daughters</u> of one <u>mother</u>,
That Mother <u>only</u> <u>Sister</u> to the <u>Marquesse</u>,

Whose charge hath since her death (being

    left a widdow)

Here in this place prefer'd your education.   10

Is't so?

    Cla.   It is even so, and howsoever

Report may wander loosely in some scandall

Against our privacies; yet we have wanted

No gracefull meanes fit for our births and qualities,

68 To traine us up into a vertuous knowledge

Of what, and who we ought to be.

    Flo.   Our Uncle

Hath often told us, how it more concern'd him

Before he shew'd us to the world, to render

Our youths and our demeanors in each action

Approv'd by his experience, then too early

Adventure on the follies of the age,

By prone temptations fatall.

    Sil.   In good deed la,

We meane no harme.

    Cas.   Deceit must want a shelter

Under a roofe that's covering to soules   24

So white as breaths beneath it, such as these

    are.   25

My happines shares largely in this blessing,

And I must thanke direction of the providence

Which led me hither.

    <u>Cla</u>.   Aptly have you stil'd it,

A providence. For ever in chast loves,   29

Such majestie hath power. ---- Our Kinsman

    <u>Troylo</u>   30

Was herein his owne factor; he will prove,

Beleeve him Lady, every way as constant,

As noble. We can baile him from the cruelty   33

Of misconstruction.

    <u>Flo</u>.   You will find his tongue

But a just Secretary to his heart.

    <u>Cas</u>.   The Guardianesse

(Deare Creatures) now and then, it seemes

Makes bold to talke.

    <u>Cla</u>.   Sh'as waited on us

From all our Cradles, will prate sometimes odly,

However meanes but sport; I am unwilling

Our houshold should breake up, but must obey

His wisedome, under whose command we live.   41

Sever our companies I'm sure we shall not;

Yet 'tis a pretty life this and a quiet.

69 Enter Morosa, Secco, his apron on, Bason of water,
        Scissors, Combe, Towels, Razor, etc.

Sec. Chuck, duckling, honye, mouse, monkey all and every thing; I am thine ever and only,
will never offend againe, as I hope to shave
cleane and get honour by't. Heartily I aske   47
forgivenesse; bee gracious to thine owne flesh
and blood, and kisse me home.

Mor. Looke you provoke us no more, for
this time you shall finde mercy. -- Was't that   51
hedgehog set thy braines a crowing? Bee quits   52
with him, but doe not hurt the great male-baby.

Sec. Enough, I am wise, and will be merry. --   54
Hast Beauties, the Caroches will sodaine receive yee; a night of pleasure is toward. Pray   56
for good husbands a peece, that may trim you
neatly, (dainty ones) and let mee alone to trim   58
them.

Mor. Loving hearts be quick as soone as
ye can. Time runs apace; what you must doe, doe   61
nimbly, and give your minds to't. Young bloods   62
stand fumbling? Fie away, be ready for shame be-   63
fore-hand. Husband, stand to thy tackling hus-   64
band like a man of mettall: goe, goe, goe.

                              Exit Morosa and Ladies.

Sec. Will ye come away loyterers? Shall I   66
wait all day? Am I at livery d'ye thinke.

Enter Spadone ready to be trim'd, and Nitido.

<u>Spa</u>. Here and ready; what a mouthing thou

keep'st. I have but scour'd my hands, and cur-   69

ried my head to save time. Honest <u>Secco</u>, neat   70

<u>Secco</u>, precious barbarian, now thou lookst like

a worshipfull Tooth-drawer; would I might see   72

thee on horsebacke, in the pompe once.

<u>Sec</u>. A Chaire, a Chaire, quick, quick.

<u>Nit</u>. Here's a chaire, a chaire politique,

my fine boy. Sit thee downe in triumph, and rise   76

one of the nine Worthies; thou'lt be a sweet youth

anon sirrah.

<u>Spa</u>. So, to worke with a grace now, I can-·

not but highly be in love with the fashion of

70 Gentry, which is never compleat, till the <u>snip</u>

<u>snap</u> of dexterity, hath mow'd off the excrements

of slovenry.

<u>Sec</u>. Very commodiously deliver'd I protest.

<u>Nit</u>. Nay, the thing under your fingers is a

<u>whelpe</u> <u>of</u> <u>the</u> <u>wits</u>, I can assure you.   86

<u>Spa</u>. I a whelpe of the wits? No, no, I   87

cannot barke impudently, and ignorantly enough;

---- oh, and a man of this Art had now and then

Soveraigntie over faire Ladies, you would tickle

their <u>upper</u> and their <u>lower</u> <u>lips</u>, you'd so smouch
and belaver their chopps.

    <u>Sec</u>. We light on some offices for Ladies
too, as occasion serves.

    <u>Nit</u>. Yes, frizzle or pouder their haire,
plane their eye-browes, set a napp on their cheekes,
keepe secrets, and tell newes; that's all.

    <u>Sec</u>. Winke fast with both your eyes. The   98
ingredients to the composition of this ball, are
most odorous Camphire, pure sope of <u>Venice</u>, oyle
of sweet Almonds, with the spirit of Allome; they
will search and smart shrewdly, if you keep not
the shop-windowes of your head close.

    <u>Spa</u>. Newes? Well remember'd, that's part   104
of your trade too. (Prethee doe not rub so roughly.) 105
And how goes the tattle o'th'towne? What novel-   106
ties stirring, ha?

    <u>Sec</u>. Strange, and scarse to be credited; a
gelding was lately seene to leape an old Mare;
and an old man of one hundred and twelve stood
in a white sheet for getting a wench of fifteene
with childe, here hard by. Most admirable and   112
portentous.

    <u>Spa</u>. Ile never beleeve it. 'Tis impossible.   114
    <u>Nit</u>. Most certaine, some <u>Doctor</u> <u>Farriers</u>

are of the opinion that the Mare may cast a Foale,

which the Master of their Hall conclude in spight

of all Jockies and their familiars, will carry

every race before him, without spurre or switch.

    Spa. O rare, a man might venture ten or

twenty to one safely then, and ne're be in dan-   121

71 ger o' the cheate. ---- This water me thinks is   122

none of the sweetest; Camphire and soape of

Venice say ye.

    Sec. With a little grecum album for mun-

dification.

    Nit. Grecum album is a kinde of white per-

fum'd pouder, which plaine Countrey people, I

beleeve, call dog-muske.

    Spa. Dog-muske, poxe o'the dog-muske!   130

What dost meane to bleach my nose, thou giv'st

such twitches to't? Set me at liberty as soone   132

as thou canst, gentle Secco.

    Sec. Onely pare off a little superfluous

downe from your chin, and all's done.

    Spa. Pish, no matter for that. Dispatch,   136

I entreat thee.

    Nit. Have patience man; 'tis for his credit

to be neat.   139

    Spa. What's that so cold at my throat, and

scrubs so hard?

Sec. A kinde of steele instrument ycleped
a Razor, a sharp toole and a keene. It has a   143
certaine vertue of cutting a throat, if a man
please to give his mind to't; ---- hold up your
muzzle Signior. ---- When did you talke baudily   146
to my wife last? Tell me for your owne good   147
(Signior) I advise you.

Spa. I talke baudily to thy wife? Hang   149
baudry; good now mind thy busines, lest thy hand
slip.

Nit. Give him kinde words you were best,
for a toy that I know.

Sec. Confesse, or I shall marre your grace
in whiffing Tobacco or squirting of sweet wines
downe your gullet. ---- You have beene offering   156
to play the gelding we told yee of I suppose;
---- speake truth. (Move the semicircle of your   158
countenance to my left hand side.) Out with the   159
truth; would you have had a leap?   160

Nit. Spadone, thou art in a lamentable
pickle. Have a good heart and pray if thou canst. 162
I pitty thee.

Spa. I protest and vow friend Secco, I
know no leaps, I.

    Sec. Letcherously goatish and an Eunuch?

This cutt, and then ----   167

72   Spa. Confound thee, thy leaps and thy cuts,

I am no Eunuch, you finicall asse! I am no   169

Eunuch; but at all points as well provided, as

any he in Italy, and that thy Wife could have

told thee. This your conspiracie, to thrust my   172

head into a brazen tub of Kitchin-lee, hud-winke

mine eyes in mud-soape, and then offer to cut my

throat in the darke like a Coward? I may live to

be reveng'd on both of yee.

    Nit. Oh, scurvy! thou art angry! Feele   177

man whether thy weason be not cracked first.

    Sec. You must fiddle my braines into a

jealousie, rub my temples with saffron, and

burnish my forehead with the juyce of yellowes!   181

Have I fitted yee now sir?

                  Enter Morosa.

    Spa. All's whole yet I hope?

    Mor. Yes, sirrah; all is whole yet; but if

ever thou dost speak treason against my sweeting

and me once more, thoul't finde a roguy bargaine

on't. <u>Deare</u>, this was handled like one of spirit   187

and discretion. <u>Nitido</u> has pag'd it trimly too.   188

No wording, but make ready and attend at Court.

    <u>Sec</u>. Now we know thou art a man; we for-

get what hath past, and are fellowes and friends

againe.

    <u>Nit</u>. Wipe your face cleane; and take heed

of a Razor.

    <u>Spa</u>. The feare put me into a sweat; I can-

not helpe it; I am glad I have my throat mine

owne, and must laugh for Company, or be laught at.

                    All Exit.   06

[V. iii)

        Enter Livio, and Troylo.

    <u>Liv</u>. You finde Sir, I have prov'd a ready

    servant,

And brought th' expected guests, amidst these

    feastings,

These costly entertainments; you must pardon

My incivility that here sequesters

Your eares from choise of musique, or discourse

To a lesse pleasant parley. Night drawes on,   6

And quickly will grow old; it were unmanly

For any Gentleman, who loves his honour,

73 To put it on the rack. Here is small comfort   9
Of such a satisfaction as was promis'd,
Though certainly it must be had. Pray tell me   11
What can appeare about me to be us'd thus?
My soule is free from injuries.

    <u>Troy</u>.   My tongue   13
From serious untruths. I never wrong'd you,   14
Love you too well to meane it now.

    <u>Liv</u>.   Not wrong'd mee!   15
(Blest Heaven!) This is the bandie of a patience   16
Beyond all sufferance.

    <u>Troy</u>. If your owne acknowledgement
Quit me not fairely ere the houres of rest
Shall shut our eyes up, say I made a forfeit
Of what no length of yeares can once redeeme.

    <u>Liv</u>. Fine whirles in tame imagination; on
    sir,
It is scarce mannerly at such a season,
Such a solemnitie (the place and presence
Consider'd) with delights, to mixe combustions.

    <u>Troy</u>. Prepare for free contents, and give
    'em welcome.   25

Flourish. Enter Octavio, Julio, Flavia, Rom-
    anello, Camillo and Vespuci.

    <u>Oct</u>. I dare not study words, or hold a
complement
For this particular; this speciall favour.
    <u>Jul</u>. Your bounty and your love, my Lord,
must justly
Ingage a thankfulnes.

    <u>Fla</u>.   Indeede
Varieties of entertainment heere
Have so exceeded all account of plentie,
That you have left (great Sir) no rareties
Except an equall welcome which may purchase
Opinion of a common Hospitality.
    <u>Oct</u>. But for this grace (Madam) I will
lay open
Before your judgements which I know can rate
'em,
A Cabinet of Jewels, rich and lively.   37
The world can shew none goodlier; those I prize
Deare as my life. ---- Nephew ----

74   <u>Troy</u>.   Sir, I obey you. ----   39
                         Exit Troylo.   03

    <u>Fla</u>. Jewels, my Lord.
    <u>Oct</u>.   No strangers eye e're view'd them,40
Unlesse your Brother <u>Romanello</u> haply
Was wo'd unto a sight for his approvement:

No more.

    <u>Rom</u>.   Not I, I doe protest; I hope Sir

You cannot thinke I am a lapidarie.   44

I skill in Jewels?

    <u>Oct</u>.   'Tis a proper quality

For any Gentleman; your other friends

May be are not so coy.

    <u>Jul</u>.   Who they? They know not   47

A <u>Topaze</u> from an <u>Opall</u>.

    <u>Cam</u>.   We are ignorant

In gems which are not common.

    <u>Ves</u>.   But his Lordship

Is pleas'd (it seemes) to try our ignorance.

For passage of the time, till they are brought,

Pray looke upon a Letter lately sent me.   52

Lord <u>Julio</u>, (Madam) <u>Romanello</u>, read

A noveltie; 'tis written from <u>Bonony</u>.   54

<u>Fabricio</u> once a Merchant in this Citie

Is enter'd into orders, and receiv'd

Amongst the Capuchins a fellow, newes

Which ought not any way to be unpleasant.   58

Certaine I can assure it.

    <u>Jul</u>.   He at last has

Bestow'd himselfe upon a glorious service.

    <u>Rom</u>. Most happie man, I now forgive the

          injuries

Thy former life expos'd thee to.

          Liv.   Turne Capuchine,

Hee, whiles I stand a Cypher and fill up

Only an uselesse summe to be laid out

In an unthrifty lewdnesse, that must buy   65

Both name and riot. Oh my fickle destinie!   66

75   Rom. Sister, you cannot taste this course

          but bravely,

But thankfully.

          Fla.   Hee's now dead to the world

And lives to heaven; a Saints reward reward him.   69

[Aside] My onely lov'd Lord, all your feares

          are henceforth

Confin'd unto a sweet and happie pennance.

Enter Troylo, Castamela, Clarella, Floria, Silvia,

     and Morosa.

          Oct. Behold, I keepe my word. These are

          the Jewels   72

Deserve a treasurie; I can be prodigall

Amongst my friends. Examine well their lustre.   74

Do's it not sparkle? Wherefore dwels your silence 75

In such amazement?

    <u>Liv</u>. [Aside]   Patience keepe within me.   76
Leap not yet rudely into scorne of anger.

    <u>Fla</u>. Beauties incomparable.

    <u>Oct</u>.   <u>Romanello</u>,
I have beene onely Steward to your pleasures;
You lov'd this Ladie once. What say you now
    to her?   80

    <u>Cas</u>. I must not court you Sir.

    <u>Rom</u>.   By no meanes faire one.   81
Enjoy your life of greatnesse; sure the spring
Is past; the Bowers Of Fancies is quite wither'd   83
And offer'd like a lottery to be drawne;
I dare not venture for a blanke. Excuse me, ---- 85
Exquisite Jewels.

    <u>Liv</u>.   Hearke ye <u>Troylo</u>.

    <u>Troy</u>.   Spare me.

    <u>Oct</u>. You then renounce all right in <u>Cas</u>-
    tamela?   87
Say <u>Romanello</u>.

    <u>Rom</u>.   Gladly.

    <u>Troy</u>.   Then I must not;
Thus I embrace mine owne, my wife; confirme it.
Thus when I faile (my dearest) to deserve thee
Comforts and life shall faile me.

     Cas.   Like vow I, for my part.

76   Troy. Livio, now my Brother, justly   92
I have given satisfaction.

     Cas.   Oh excuse
Our secrecie; I have beene ----

     Liv.   Much more worthy   94
A better Brother, he a better Friend
Then my dull braines could fashion.

     Rom.   Am I cosen'd.

     Oct. You are not Romanello; we examin'd
On what conditions your affections fix'd,
And found them meerely Courtship; but my

     Nephew
Lov'd with a faith resolv'd, and us'd his policie
To draw the Ladie into this societie,
More freely to discover his sinceritie
Even without Livio's knowledge; thus succeeded   103
And prospered. He's my heire and she deserv'd
     him.   104

     Jul. Storme not at what is past.

     Fla.   A fate as happie
May crowne you with a full content.

     Oct.   What ever
Report hath talk'd of me abroad, and these,   107
Know they are all my neeces, are the daughters

To my dead onely Sister; this their Guardianesse   109
Since they first saw the World.   Indeed my Mis-
    tresses   110
They are.   I have none other.   How brought up   111
Their qualities may speake.   Now <u>Romanello</u>,   112
And Gentlemen, for such I know yee all,
Portions they shall not want both fit and worthy;
Nor will I looke on fortune.   If you like   115
Court them and win them; here is free accesse,   116
In mine owne Court henceforth.   Only for thee   117
<u>Livio</u> I wish <u>Clarella</u> were alotted.

    <u>Liv</u>.   Most noble Lord, I am struck silent.

    <u>Fla</u>.   Brother, heere's noble choyce.

    <u>Rom</u>.   Frenzy, how didst thou seize me!

    <u>Cla</u>.   We knew you Sir, in <u>Prugniolo's</u>
    posture.

77   <u>Flo</u>.   Were merry at the sight.

    <u>Sil</u>.   And gave you welcome.

    <u>Mor</u>.   Indeed forsooth, and so we did an't
    like ye.

    <u>Oct</u>.   Enough, enough; now to shut up the
    night,
Some meniall servants of mine owne are ready
For to present a merriment; they intend
Acording to th' occasion of the meeting,

In severall shapes to shew how love oreswayes

All men of severall conditions; <u>Soldier</u>,

<u>Gentry</u>, <u>foole</u>, <u>scholler</u>, <u>Merchant</u> <u>man</u>, and

    <u>Clowne</u>.   131

A harmlesse recreation; take your places. ----

                <u>Dance</u>.

Your duties are perform'd. Henceforth, <u>Spadone</u>,   133

Cast off thy borrow'd title. Nephew <u>Troylo</u>,   134

His <u>Mother</u> gave thee suck; esteeme him honestly.

    Lights for the Lodgings, 'tis high time for rest;

    <u>Great</u> <u>men</u> may be mistooke when they meane best.

               FINIS.

Epilogue.

Mor. A While suspected (Gentlemen) I looke
For no new Law, being quitted by the
Booke.

Cla. Our harmelesse pleasure's, free in
every sort
Actions of scandall; may they free
report.

Cas. Distrust is base, presumption urgeth
wrongs;
But noble thoughts must prompt as
noble tongues.

Fla. Fancie and Judgement are a Playes
full matter:
If we have er'd in one, right you
the latter.

CHAPTER FOUR

A NOTE TO THE APPENDICES

The numbering of the preceding text has been designed to facilitate the use of the following appendices
and to assist in any possible reconstruction of the
Quarto. Thus the text contains two sets of numbers, one
to its left and the other to its right. The former runs
consecutively from 1-77, and indicates those lines which
begin a new page of the Quarto. The latter, which indicates the line numbers, runs consecutively from the beginning to the end of each scene, with the exception that
stage directions are numbered separately and are always
preceded in the notes and in the text by a zero. Following the usual procedure of modern editions, prose is
numbered according to each typed line, poetry according
to each verse line. Where a verse line is split between
two or more characters it is appropriately indented. Any
line with a number to its right indicates the presence of
an emendation as recorded in the textual notes.

In Appendix A, the explanatory notes, a gloss is included for virtually all the many slang and obsolete terms
found in the text. The authority for most of these glosses
is the Old English Dictionary. In addition, critical and
interpretive notes are furnished where appropriate.

Unlike the textual notes, no key in the text alerts the reader to the existence of an explanatory note for any particular word, phrase, or passage. To incorporate such keys for both explanatory and textual notes would have cluttered the text, and since the principal purpose of this work is to provide a critical rather than a reading text, the textual notes were given priority.

Appendix B, the textual notes, lists first the reading of this text followed by a bracket (]), and then the reading of the Quarto. In some cases, where this text uses the readings of previous editions, the bracket has been followed by the appropriate siglum, W, G, and/or D, to indicate respectively the editions of Weber, Gifford, and Gifford-Dyce. This procedure, however, has been used only with substantive variants and ignores all accidentals. For example, in line number 16 of the Prologue Gifford uses the word "own," but does not put it in italics. The entry in Appendix B for this item would not indicate Gifford's use of roman type, and should be taken only to mean that Gifford is in substantial agreement with the present text. All variants spread over two or more lines are identified by the line number on which the necessary lemma begins. The presence of a slash (/) indicates the end of a typed line for this text and printed line for the Quarto. An effort has been made to confine each entry to a single variant. However, this has often proved impractical, especially where this text emends to a full stop, thus forcing a following capital.

Appendix C, the historical çollation, lists <u>substantive</u> variants between the present text, the Quarto, and the nineteenth century texts of Weber, Gifford and Gifford-Dyce. In each case the first entry is the reading of the present text. It is followed by either an appropriate siglum(s) and/or by further entries to reflect the readings of the other editions. Though their inclusion is arguable, variant forms such as "you," "ye," "yee" and "he," "hee," "a'" have been listed here principally in the hope that they may be of some use in any study of the general habits of the various editors. Finally, where a substantive variant exists between only some of the texts, the exact readings of all of the texts have been provided, even though some will differ from others only in accidentals. In such a short list this longer but exact method seems preferable to merely indicating general agreement.

Appendix D contains four charts which are self-explanatory. It is hoped that their inclusion will assist anyone who wishes to closely examine the Quarto.

Appendix A

Explanatory Notes

The Epistle Dedicatorie

1.   Lord MackDonnell: identified in Weber's edition as a supporter of Charles I.

10. not . . . aym'd at any thrift: No reward is expected for the dedication which is given freely to a worthy person. Such independence is typical of Ford.

13-17.   Endeavor . . . allowance: Ford argues it is not presumptious of him to dedicate the work to MackDonnell, a man he had never met, as his only motive is to honor the Lord's well known reputation for virtue.

18. generall suffrage: public approbation.

20. this . . . presentment: the dedication.

22. construction: company

To Master John Ford

1.   To Master etc.: These commendatory verses seem to be an attack on the contemporary fashion for well off amateurs of both the University and Court to finance the sometimes lavish productions of their own too often eminently forgettable plays. Thus Greenfield protests he writes at his "owne charges," i.e., he is not being paid for his praise, rather his praise is paid to one of the "right Poets," not a "counterfeit" or one of the "new Pretenders."

1.   middle Temple: in London, a residence for students of the law.

9-14.   These . . . faire: an unusual commendation for what in the play is a supposed seraglio.

10. itch: sexual

13. relish't: enjoyed or understood, with a double
entendre.

13. repayre: reside.

21. Edw. Greenfield: probably one of Ford's London
friends. See Bentley, Jacobean and Caroline Stage, III,
437.

Prologue

Siena: town in Tuscany, Italy.

1-16. The Fancies . . . paines: Ewing (Burtonian Melancholy in the Plays of John Ford, pp. 28-32) argues that
the Prologue was written only at the time of publication
and that it is Ford's reply to supposed ridicules directed
at The Fancies by Shirley in his Changes, or Love in a
Maze.

1-10. The Fancies . . . by him: Ford claims the play is
a product of his own originality, a claim true of the plot
but not so true of the characters who include many recog-
nizable types.

5. locke: love-lock.

11. His: the author's.

11. conceit: to imagine or to fancy.

13-14. traduc'd . . . home: a satiric reply to any would-
be critics.

16. Fancie: imagine, with a pun on both Octavio's bower
and the title of the play.

16. Fancie . . . paines: apparently an allusion to what
Ford knows will be the inevitable, but incorrect, conclusion of his audience as to the nature of the Fancies,
i.e., Octavio's bower.

I. i

1-10. Doe . . . not?: Troylo satirically admonishes

Livio to try to furnish his tables, fill his coffers, and
add to his titles with naught but the coin of his reputation.

3.   trim your <u>liveries</u>: dress your servants.

18.   compast: achieved.

18-22. Wherein . . . it?: wealth and its natural accom-
paniment--greatness--shield those who possess them from
all censure save one's own conscience.

22.   it: greatness.

30.   <u>Ligorne</u>: Leghorn, on the coast in Tuscany, not far
from both Siena and Florence.

36.   Chamlet: camlet, a fine fabric made of angora during
the sixteenth and seventeenth centuries.

48.   dispensation: a release from her marriage to Fabricio
on the basis of a pre-contract; see Introduction, p. 30.

51.   disease: melancholy; see Introduction, p. 13.

65.   preferment: advancement or promotion.

68.   Tissue: a rich fabric.

70.   cunning: skill.

73-77.   A way . . . on't?: Troylo implies there is a way
for Livio to both pander his sister and simultaneously
guard her chastity.

107-113. Is not . . . shares: it is better to obtain preferment from the Lord than to spend months waiting for
handouts from the Lord's servants.

108. at livory: with the servants.

110. Arras: tapestry.

111. Usher: doorkeeper who controls access to the Lord's
chambers.

115. expectation: anticipation of preferment.

116. for attendance: in effect, for doing one's duty.

123. from goodnesse: on the basis of goodness.

126-127. speake . . . Batchelor: commend Octavio to my sister.

131. Stand ingenious: be aware, perceptive, or sensitive.

I. ii

01. Castingbottle: for sprinkling; Secco is a barber and carries his tools with him.

03. Girdle: waist or belt.

28. Codled: pampered.

28. parcell: part.

29. markes: teeth.

31. Posset: hot, spiced and sweetened milk curdled with ale or wine.

37. make thee a man: Spadone, a supposed eunuch, takes this as a jibe at his condition.

39. prickeard: perhaps with hair cut short in the manner of the Puritans.

39. foyst: pickpocket.

39. citterne: a pearshaped guitar with grotesquely carved head, often kept in barber shops for the amusement of customers.

40. gew, gaw: gewgaw, a trifle.

40. knacke: a con-man.

40. snipper-snapper: a conceited fellow.

41. decrements of my pendants: loss of my testicles.

43. Dowsets: testicles.

44. Cuckold: a husband whose wife has been unfaithful;

according to folklore such a husband grows horns on his
forehead.

45. checker: a fault finder.

56. camphire Balls: camphor, once supposed an aphrodisiac.

82. Pap and Bulbeefe: pablum and tough beef with probable
pun on teat and penis.

94. gambos: leaps or skips.

108. moyle: mule.

111. crimpe: The OED cites this apparently derisive use
of the term but can only list its meaning as "doubtful."

115. lib'd breech: a reference to Spadone's supposed
castrated condition.

117. crosse tree: gallows.

118. wag-halter-Page: a witty page destined for the hang-
man's noose or halter.

119. Satire: Satyr.

I. iii

5. expectation: promise.

6. example: model or perfection.

6-9. but Sir . . . consideration: "Our small fortunes
must make you construe [conster] gently my refusal of you
[forbearance] as the proper thing to do under the circumstances."

22-24. to force . . . love of want: a confusing passage,
but apparently the intended meaning is love and poverty
do not mix.

39. Caroach: a luxurious coach.

39. guarded: richly and ornamentedly clothed.

47. distractions: annoyances or perturbations.

49. bait: exasperate or damage.

66. scholler: Romanello is a student and apparently a
young man; see III. iii. 6.

75. purchase: the annual return on property which might
be acquired in a dowry.

78. Endevours and an active braine: Energy and intelligence.

79. patrimonies: not merely wealth, but name, reputation,
and, in short, one's entire heritage.

81. game: targets or marks.

82. haire: strength, by analogy with Sampson's.

90. scambling: to get somehow.

95. Conceives: imagines.

95. Philosophers stone: the substance long sought by al-
chemists to turn base metals to gold.

96. Indies: source of wealth.

109-110. Then . . . price: "nothing is of any value until
it is marketed."

116. competency: worth.

118. So . . . void: "Your efforts will be fruitless."

118. aquittance: release.

122. the treasure . . . open'd: Castamela's newly bloomed
beauty.

124-126: My . . . perfection: "My jealousy caused me to
fear nurturing your growth too cautiously."

127. perish: to use up, i.e., to completely capture;
see IV. i. 79 for similar use of the word.

141. neat cloath'd: well expressed.

145. pretty: used ironically.

153-154: I . . . mine: Castamela may be being deliberately

ambiguous; not unlike Hamlet's "my thanks are too dear a
halfpenny."

161-162. Now . . . once: Such lines as these seem a deliberate effort on Ford's part to deceive his audience.

168. Usher: attendant.

177. Or . . . or: either . . . or.

II. i.

01. supported: accompanied, probably on their arms.

14. play day: probably Lord Mayor's day.

14. Pageants: flags associated with the procession and
shows of Lord Mayor's day and other festivals.

17. eat our viands: dine with us.

32. pettish: peevish.

33. toysome: playful or whimsical.

34. breeding: being well brought up with pun on possible
pregnancy.

35. Long . . . now: Flavia suggests she has the unusual
cravings traditionally ascribed to pregnant women.

42. swab: behave rudely.

46. briefe: argument or contents.

47. last: possibly a misprint for "lost" or perhaps the
sense is "the last fortune I can hope to achieve."

49. Wittol: a complaisant cuckold.

51. gaine: cuckoldry, used ironically.

59. Venus Cat: This may be an allusion to the occasional
association of Venus with the Egyptian moon god Isis who,
in turn, was frequently coalesced with Bast, the consort
of the sun god Ra, who was always portrayed with the head

of a cat. The rest of the line - "man chang'd into a woman"
- may allude to the practice observed in Vergil's Aeneid of
man making sacrifice to Venus as Luna [Isis], the moon,
while they were dressed in women's clothing, and of women
making sacrifice while they were dressed in men's clothing.
Certainly such an allusion would be appropriate to the
moral and ethical situation in which Fabricio and Flavia
find themselves.

60. enbleme: emblem, a symbol or sign.

61. Acteon . . . cloth: Acteon gazing on the naked Artemus. Acteon was subsequently torn to pieces by his own
hounds after Artemus had turned him into a stag.

63. Scrivener: scribe.

64. Is . . . learned: Flavio accuses Fabricio of not
having the legal counsel he apparently claims, but having
only the scribe.

76. twangs roundly: resounds soundly.

81. leisure: opportunity.

83. vowes: marriage vows.

89. warrantable: good and true.

94. The last of my decayes: "my final impoverishment."

98. meane: moderate.

101. Without controule: freely, without need for force or
constraint.

110. precontract: Fabricio claimed that a formal betrothal between Flavia and another, not Julio, invalidated the
subsequent marriage between himself and Flavia. Obviously
Fabricio's claim was made for a price. For a review of
this problem see the Blayney article cited in the bibliography and discussed in Chapter One of this text.

120-122. But . . . purchase: "If I had succumbed to his
blandishments we would not have been separated from each
other by his money." It is not clear if Flavia is speaking
hypothetically or if Julio did try to seduce her.

126. antique carriage: antic or strange behaviour. An

example of such deliberately artificial behaviour is seen
in the opening segment of this scene where Flavia uses it
to deceive Camillo and Vespuci of her true feelings.

128. Keepe those Duccats: Flavia apparently hands Fabricio money.

129. bravery: something to be proud of; used ironically.

133. goodnesse: Gifford feels this is a misprint caused
by the "goodnesse" in the preceding line. He emends to
"sadness" as offering what may have been Ford's meaning.
Gifford may be correct, but the quarto was very carefully
printed, and "goodnesse" does make some sense in the line.
Flavia may be expressing a resolve to quietly lead an
honorable life despite the wagging tongues of such as
Camillo, Vespuci, and others.

137. Ile . . . supplies: "I'll supply your needs."

138-139. I . . . owne: "I must not remember what once
was."

139. Keepe . . . distance: Apparently Flavia and Fabricio
have drawn close together during this scene.

141. cast familier: rejected friend, probably said with
intended contempt.

142. Wambles: turns queasy.

145. companion: Fabricio; said with contempt.

152. thing: Fabricio.

162. som countrey: England and the court of Charles II.

II. ii

2. Calenture: fever.

10. bare: simple or mere.

10. grounds: destroy, as in a ship run aground; Livio is
continuing the sea voyage metaphor used by Troylo.

13. Neate attendance: elegant and assiduous servants.

17. Might . . . conceit: "Live into one's old age contemplating the wonders here."

21. invite to: bring on or yield to.

55. cunning: able.

56. abilities: faculties or gifts.

58. Or . . . with: "Or what he gives out of a sense of either obligation or munificence."

76. choices: girls.

78. meanely: Low born.

88. head-ach: caused by wearing or in this case fear of wearing the cuckold's horns.

88. Yellowes: jealousy, caused by choler, one of the four humours.

95. 'Tis ominous in nature: Livio suggests Troylo is a threat to cuckold his uncle, Octavio.

104. wedding: between Secco and Morosa.

108. studied: observed.

111. him: Octavio.

112. game: of love.

116. taken: pleased.

03. Enter . . . : musicians also enter; see line 201 following.

127. prostitute: devote, with a double entendre.

128. bounties: virtues.

131. Cattamountaine: Leopard or panther.

137. Touch hole: the hole in a gun's breech through which the charge is ignited; here with bawdy innuendo.

145. moyle: mule.

146. ring'd mare: a mare so fitted with metal rings as to prevent her from being bred.

146. burthens: used in double sense of "burthen" as "re-frain" or "retort" and "burthen" as "load."

148. shey: a possible misprint for hey or say.

178-179. Sure . . . Licorice: "You have some youth left," but with a pun on "Liquorish" or "lecherous."

181. rubs: impediments.

186. eare-wig: parasite.

187. fit: madden.

187. 'em: Secco.

188. My . . . sever: In this brief exchange, as elsewhere in the play, the audience is given only partial informa-tion. Apparently Livio and Troylo have a brief private ex-change at the end of which Livio assures Troylo of some-thing. Exactly what is not clear, but almost certainly it involves "round temptation" (line 209), as Livio calls it, of Castamela.

191-192. starting hole: refuge of a hunted animal, with bawdy innuendo.

199. Buts: the cuckold's horns and objects of ridicule.

203. postures: positions.

213. They . . . pension: "to be at devotion" is "to be at one's command or service"; "to live in pension" is "to live as a boarder." Thus, the sense is "no one here has any reason to be afraid."

218. your --- / Guard me: Throughout the rest of the scene Ford allows Morosa to lead Castamela and the audi-ence to "fancy" the worst while she voices Octavio's in-nocence.

219. Genius: a powerful spirit, influential for good or evil.

227. Fond: foolish.

230. Else: otherwise.

240. deed: indeed.

241. stale: too old for marriage.

243. ruffle: paw or grope.

243. dash: confrontation.

252. put case: a legal term, the case or argument as presented to the court.

253. finde: serve or maintain.

283. As: So.

284. Free suspition: Don't worry.

287. pregnant: perceptive.

III. i

1. genius: see note for II. ii. 219.

7. politique reaches: shrewd schemes.

21. vouchsafe: bestow.

24. Fadg'd: Thrived.

25. clogs: impediments.

25. staggers: uncertainties.

28. Am . . . discovery: Nitido wants Romanello's assurance that Nitido's role in the scheme will be kept secret.

39. buffoones his complement: burlesques the Duke's behaviour.

40. According . . . season: following whatever is fashionable at the time.

45. Steletto: a pointed beard.

46. study: resolve.

47. formall foppery: foolishly excessive finery.

48. curiosity of language: strange vocabulary or figures of speech.

52. phantasticall: fantastic.

53. suppositor: inducement, from suppository; hence "physick" in the next line.

59. carriage: behaviour.

63. privilege: immunity or superiority.

67. anticke: strange or silly; see note II. i. 126.

70. pregnant: imminent.

72. Queres: questions.

74. earnest: downpayment, money.

79. inamorato: lover.

88. a': Romanello.

89. licourish: eager and, here probably, lecherous.

91-92. supposition/Strenthned by supposition: suspicion strenthened by the assumption of disguise.

93. beast it selfe: monster of jealousy.

III. ii

11. graine: dye or color.

14. over flux: overflow.

14. gall: bile; see note for II. ii. 88.

16. she: Flavia; both Camillo and Vespuci have taken

Flavia's defensive flirting seriously.

25. Piramus and Thisbe: famous mythological lovers.

26. complement: courtesy.

27. nick'd: "hit the mark."

32. goodee-madame: agreeable lady as in goodfellow.

33. compast: attained.

37. sowse: a hawk's swoop upon its prey as the prey rises in flight.

42. frail: morally weak.

43. reversioner: heir or successor.

52. best of faires: the best of the beautiful or desirable.

70. giblets: "excess baggage."

73. packs: a term of contempt for a group.

74. arrant: genuine.

91. single: honest, sincere.

92. free: liberal.

108. sadnesse: seriousness.

112. protestation: a solemn promise; the sense of the line is Julio's action - marrying Flavia - testifies to his love more than any verbal affirmation.

118. homely: familiarly; apparently an allusion to Camillo's and Vespuci's liberties.

129. Cast-away: reprobate.

III. iii

2. gamballs: leaps, physical and verbal.

5. troules: wags, rolls.

5. Mill-clack: a clapper used to shake corn from a hopper to a mill stone.

6. towzes: handles rudely.

8. Madona: Morosa.

11. Jumpe with me: "You and I are thinking the same thing."

16. page: Nitido, Troylo's page.

16. go to: an expression of disapproval.

18. geere: business.

19. Brokage: pandering.

20. Bulchin: bull calf.

21. rore: exchange, barter; Spadone means exchange mates.

24. Let . . . forehead: Spadone feels for the cuckold's horns.

30. Velvet tips: first growth of a buck's horns.

31. hart: a pun on "hart" as "courage" and as "deer."

38. trim: beat.

38. tram: one of the upright legs of a gallows, but also the shafts, always in at least pairs, of a cart, barrow, wheelbarrow, etc. Secco seems to have the former in mind, while in the next line Spadone seems to make a sexual joke on the latter.

46. Mountbanking: deceitful.

46. foyst: rogue; see note for I. ii. 39.

47. pretender: wooer, suitor.

53. Metamorphosed: Since Spadone is impotent, it would require a metamorphosis for him to "drive a trade."

58. fegaries: whims.

59. tame Antick: meek grotesque; grotesque presumably because of the horns.

62. fellow: peer.

66. Gip: an expression of anger and/or contempt.

70. These exchanges among Secco, Spadone, and Morosa apparently go on independently of the rest of the action on the stage involving Troylo, Romanello, and the Fancies.

72. treedle: Gifford glosses this as "street walker" by an analogy with "the part of the loom on which the foot presses"; the OED gives "whore" as one meaning by an analogy with the use of the word to describe "The action of the male bird in coition." However a more probable meaning is "sheep dung." Admittedly, the difference hardly matters.

73. Cat a Mountaine: leopard or panther; see note for II. ii. 131.

83. trim: fine.

86. Baboon: Morosa; apparently Morosa has implicated Spadone in the possible cuckolding of Secco.

87-88. Keepe/your bow close: Remaine chaste.

89. Beshrew: Curse.

92. bob: cut.

93. Spruice: brisk and/or dapper.

97. Tho . . . out: "Though a woman with several lovers would make any one of her lovers extremely jealous."

98. pumpe: struggle.

102. resolutions: judgements.

103. phlegmatick: sluggish or apathetic.

106-116. That . . . females: Romanello suggests a woman betrays her disposition in her dress.

108. Points: the laces used to secure the bodice.

111. rides the Cock-horse: is high-spirited.

113. fish daies: days of abstinence.

115. pudder: fuss.

117-118. Else . . . profit: Clarella concludes Silvia's
line in an ironic vein.

117. they: men.

117. sots: fools.

122. shaver: barber, swindler, or wag; all three OED
meanings are applicable in the context.

124. knacks: deceits.

125. troules: wags, rolls; see note for III. iii. 5.

127. Cuckolds livory: horns.

128. Philosophic: reason.

141. Cokes: fool.

142-143. Whope . . . Woman: See The Winter's Tale,
IV. iv. 2024, First Folio.

149. broad: out-spoken.

161. service: as in "I am at your service."

171. single: simple.

172. brook'd: enjoyed.

175. resolution: determination, answer.

177. surquedry: arrogance.

179. protestation: a solemn promise, presumably of
suitors; see note for III. ii. 112.

183. trewanting: truanting.

199. should: would.

200. entertainment: request.

203-205. Love . . . belov'd: for a discussion of this
well known passage see Chapter One, pp. 28-29.

208. fresh: newly arrived and unsullied.

210. boast: extol.

213. constant: faithful.

218. awful: profound.

221. factresse: agent.

221. tampering: scheming.

226. Spannell: fawning.

230. proffer: offer.

230. courtesie: welcome, invitation.

236. by: in.

239. statist: statesman.

243-245. Convert . . . there: Castamela pleads with
Octavio to maintain his Fancies openly and honorably in
his court.

256-257. Be . . . lent: This exchange will be kept secret.

263. inck'd: Dyce emends to nick'd, meaning "won." This
emendation is probably correct.

IV. i

3. spheare: of Octavio and his Fancies; Castamela is
deliberately baiting Livio.

8. Demeane your carriage: Beare yourself with humility.

11. observe: respect.

15. trimme: fashion, mode, i.e., one of the Fancies.

16. Port: bearing.

20. brave it: carry it off.

21-23. Love . . . belov'd: Castamela deliberately mimics
Octavio; see III. iii. 203-205.

28. conceit: image.

29. contemplation: thought.

36. swindge: freedom or sway.

38. service: a servile position.

40. thrifty: successful.

41. Want: Lack.

52. mew'd up: confined.

52. lure: cord, chain; both this and the preceding
"mew'd" are derived from falconry.

54. promise past: presumably to Octavio.

62. memorie: reputation.

63. confidence: trust.

68. plurisie: excess.

87. distrust: doubt.

105-113. Incomparable . . . him: This is an allusive exchange between Castamela and Troylo. Apparently Castamela
has been acting upon the advice of Troylo, advice to which
the audience is not privy. This seems the implication of
Castamela's use of "Counsellor," of Troylo's reassurance
of her fears (ll. 106-108), and of Castamela's resolve to
accept on faith - "credulous" - Troylo's nobility despite
the conflict between her language, spoken according to
Troylo's advice, and her heart.

113. quit: ease, cure.

116. Dogleech: dog veterinarian.

129. eare-wig: parasite; see note for II. ii. 186.

139. shew: perform.

144. Dog: Nitido.

144. Beare: Morosa.

148. Tospot: Drunkard.

150. Scould: Scold.

155. Let . . . now: spoken to Castamela.

160. choller: anger.

162. he: Troylo; till now Spadone has not been aware of Troylo's and Castamela's presence.

162. with a Wanion: with a vengeance.

172. Trangdidoes: the meaning is unclear, but may be a combination of either "trangam" or "twang" - both terms of contempt, and either "dido," an old story, or "dildo," phallus.

179. Coney: rabbit.

190. prick of thy weason Pipe: tongue.

191. Bodkin: a third party where there is but room for two; here in bed.

196. Alcatote: oaf.

198. Ramkin: young ram.

206. mazar: head.

207. Bedlam: lunatic.

211. Hoyday: an exclamation of surprise.

213-214. hobet a hoy: meaning is not clear but probably from "hob" for "rustic" or "clown" and "hoy," "a clumsy fellow" or "pig driver."

220. Chrisome: innocent.

220. wot: know.

222.   goose-cap: fool.

228.   Spittle: hospital for the indigent.

228.   confound: destroy.

253-254.   And . . . doe: see I. ii. 131-132.

IV. ii

4.   Caroch: a luxurious coach; see note for I. iii. 39.

9.   compos'd: elaborate, ornate, i.e., meals.

9.   Collations: repasts.

10.   surfets: feasts.

16.   Or . . . or: Either . . . or.

16.   Nature: natural affection, here between brother and sister.

18.   Not . . . ordinary: Not the usual.

19.   to chop discourses: to argue.

26.   patient: longsuffering person.

29.   No . . . liberty: Castamela asserts her new fortunes have not altered her morals.

31.   wild: unreasonable, foolish.

37.   order'd: controlled.

39.   service: duty.

45.   ward: defense, rejoinder.

50.   man: Fabricio.

53.   intrusted: i.e., by Julio.

57.   him: Julio.

62. present state: i.e., married to Julio.

76. right: justice.

87. Shall . . . distrust: Shall risk causing distrust, i.e., between Romanello and Flavia.

90. thraldome: presumably, with Castamela.

91. Novels: innovations.

103. close: secret.

104. commends: commendation.

105. Please thinke on: "It pleases you to consider."

128-129. narrowness . . . in: "our meager fortunes."

131. competencies: economic means.

132. Grave: weighty, important.

132. providence: foresight.

133. abates: falls short.

133. You use a triumph: "You exult."

136. imposture: fraud.

137. Enjoyne: Require.

137. Since . . . earnest: Since you are serious.

140. forecast: foresight.

141. recollection: presumably of his meager fortune.

141. with . . . thriftiness: a satiric reference to Livio's earlier resolve not to marry and to the basis of Livio's objections to marriage between Romanello and Castamela. See lines 145-148 following and compare with I. iii. 72-75.

150. possible: feasible.

150. answer'd: returned in kind and/or answered.

152. Creature: an unflattering allusion to Castamela.

158. <u>Titanian</u> Empire: empire of the Titans or Gods.

174. design'd: intended. This is ambiguous. Romanello means either he never intended to marry Castamela or he never conceived he would reject her as he is now; probably the latter. See line 184 following.

176. give allowance: be tolerant.

178. range: stray, here verbally.

179. Intelligence . . . swiftly: Livio realizes Romanello knows of Castamela's alliance with Octavio.

192. Questionlesse: Without doubt.

192. quit: redeem.

193. intercourse of conference: alternation or change in counsel.

194. perplext: confused.

V. i

2.   nor . . . nor: neither . . . neither.

9.   Strange: extreme, exceptional.

10-11. relish . . . nature: "enjoy the advantage of being in a nobleman's grace."

14. condition: i.e., of servants and slaves.

22. Since: Since then.

27. small-cole: charcoal.

29. custome: business, patronage.

35. Pole: barber pole, with here, as elsewhere, a double entendre.

49-51. worke . . . me: "automatically includes you in every praise or scandal which concerns me."

52. Stewardship: of the Fancies.

55. yet: still.

64. admission: to the Fancies', including Castamela's,
presence disguised as Prugnuolo.

66-67. now . . . receiv'd: now it is received as Divine
truth.

67. confirm'd: certain, assured.

67. Lady: Castamela.

88. brave: confront, challenge.

92. Parts: shares.

93. rude: ignorant. Livio implies there are legitimate
grounds for such doubts as the question raises.

97. gallant: Livio.

101. upon the sodaine: suddenly.

102. move: plead.

109. baffel'd: disgraced.

119. he: Romanello.

126. shall keepe the peace: remain undrawn.

127. alow'd: Gifford emends to "aloud," but a more likely
meaning is that of "allowed," meaning "sanctioned." Thus
Troylo would be claiming justification for an angry reply.

128. fitter: better.

V. ii

5. Patent: authority.

20. Approv'd: tested.

22. prone: easy.

31. factor: agent.

34. misconstruction: misunderstanding.

35. Guardianesse: Morosa.

53. male-baby: Nitido.

64. tackling: gear, equipment.

72. Tooth-drawer: one of a barber's duties.

72-73. would . . . once: Gifford explains this as probably
meaning "in the procession of the city 'companies of trades
and callings,' as a barber surgeon." A bawdy double entendre would not be out of character, for either Spadone or the
play.

75. politique: ingenious; the chair traps Spadone. See
The Broken Heart, IV. iv.

86. whelpe: dog, puppy; contemptuous.

90. you: i.e., such a man.

96. plane: tweeze.

101. Allome: alum.

110. an old man: Gifford sees here an allusion to Old
Parr, a man of more than one hundred years who supposedly
was rebuked by Charles I for fathering a bastard.

112. hard: close.

118. familiars: associates.

153. toy: crotchet, caprice, aversion.

173. lee: lye.

173. hud-winke: blind.

178. weason: wind pipe.

180. saffron: saffron was used to induce perspiration,
and Spadone may mean Secco has made him sweat. Saffron is
also yellowish in color, and Spadone may mean here what he
means in the next line; see following.

181. burnish . . . yellowes: "take out your jealousy on me."

182. fitted ye: taken your measure.

186. roguy: roguish, vile.

188. pag'd: attended, carried it off.

189. wording: talk.

V. iii

16. bandie: abuse.

25. free: honorable.

26. hold a complement: observe formal courtesies, here of thanks. Octavio means words and ceremony would not be sufficient to thank Julio.

28. justly: equally.

32-34. That . . . Hospitality: "All that is left for us to render you is the same welcome and hospitality you have rendered us."

42. approvement: approval, or possibly, profit.

44. lapidarie: jeweler.

54. Bonony: Bologna.

62-66. Turne . . . destinie: this is an aside.

64. laid out: paid out.

66. name: reputation.

66. riot: debauchery.

70. lov'd Lord: Fabricio.

85. blanke: ticket in the lottery.

96. cosen'd: deceived.

102. discover: reveal.

115. Nor . . . fortune: "Nor will I consider the wealth,
or poverty, of their suitors."

05. Dance: this dance or masque is possibly in imitation
of one in Davenant's Triumph of the Prince D'Amour; see
Bentley, Jacobean and Caroline Stage, III, 443-444.

Epilogue

2. quitted: acquitted.

2. Booke: the play.

3. free: devoid; takes "Actions" as object.

4. free report: absolve the reports, dishonourable, of
our actions.

APPENDIX B

TEXTUAL NOTES

[The Epistle Dedicatorie]

11. thrift;]   thrift:
13. Lordship by]   Lordship, by
15. Humility,]   Humility:
16. ungracious,]   ungracious;
19. merits. May]   merits: may
21. such]   sush
    as faithfully]   as I faithfully
    honor those]   honor, those

[To Master John Ford]

10. braines.]   braines:
18. Actors;]   Actors:

[Prologue]

3. theft. No]   theft; no
12. imaginations;]   imaginations:
15. remaines:]   remaines;
16. own opinions]GD   even opinions

[I. i]

1. manly.]   manly,

8. volume. Here's]   volume, here's
   eternity.]   eternity,
18. service. Wherein]   service, wherein
22. it?]   it.
23. wants.]   wants,
    Savelli/]   Savelli./
24. Livio.]   Livio,
28. height]   heigh
29. merrits. Well]   merrits, well
34. theft]   ieft
    was't]   waste
35. on't./]   on't/
39. Telamon, her]   Telamon her
41. employment.]   employment,
42. honour.]   honour,
43. state.]   state,
    Sienna,]   Sienna.
44. Camerine,]   Camerine.
47. purchase.]   purchase,
48. dispensation from Rome,/ Allowed]   dispensation/
                                      From Rome, allowed
49. warranted. 'Twas]   warranted: twas
54. At]   at
    best/'Tis]   best'Tis
56. honesty!]   honesty,
58. ranck, to]   ranck to
59. fee/]   fee,/
60. another-]   another,
61. society-]   society,
64. deceived.]   deceived,
65. preferment. Tis]   preferment,- tis
66. dignity.]   dignity,
67. Castamela!]   Castamela.

73. A way]   Away
76. Ivorie. Put]   Ivorie, put
    case-/]   case/
78. yours. Doe]   yours, doe
79. Nature.]   Nature,
02. Octavio]WGD Octavo
79. Be then pliable]   Q. repeats this line before
                          and after the stage direc-
                          tion. Before the stage
                          direction the line in the Q.
                          is followed by a period
                          [. . . pliable.]
80. advancement. ----]   advancement----
82. wish-/]   wish/
83. private. ----]   private----
    Sir!/]   Sir/
85. pursuit. ----]   pursuit----
    here's]   her's
87. it. You]   it, you
88. favours.]   favours,
90. it./]   it:/
94. perswadedly. ---- My]   perswadedly---- my
96. fortunes. --]   fortnnes--
    Thou]   thou
97. duty.]   duty,
99. us. [Aside] Be]   us, be
100. constant. ---- Men]   constant----men
103. supportance. While]   supportance, while
104. fall. ----]   fall----
03. Exit Octavio and Nitido.]W   Exit. Oct. Page.
107. gratitude. Is]   gratitude, is
111. Secretary,/]   Secretary/
113. shares. In]   shares, in

      all, a]   all a
      younger brother,/]   yonger brother/
116. Oft]   Of
      service- for]   service for
      attendance-/]   attendance/
117. damn'd]   damb'd
118. laughter, and]   laughter, (and
      worse, old]   worth) old
      beggerie.]   beggerie,
120. miraculous?]   miraculous.
      bargaine/]   bargaine,/
127. Batchelor. --]   Batchelor--
129. confident. The]   confident, the
131. of thy]GD   of my
      spirit. Stand]   spirit, stand
 04. Exit Troylo and Livio.]   Exeunt.

[I. ii]

  4. i'th' blood]   i'th blood
  6. perfection. --Ah]   perfection--ah
  8. yes! If]   yes, if
 12. hold! What's]   hold, what's
 13. cryer.]   cryer,
 14. lost]   Iost
      you. Heere's]   you, heere's
 17. faire. And]   faire, and
 19. owner.]   owner,
 20. meane? I'st]   meane, i'st
 21. faire?/ Be]   faire, be
 22. me. Here's]   me, here's
      duccat. Speake]   duccat, speake
 24. t'other. 'Tis]   t'other, 'tis

25. party.]   party,
26. <u>Spadone</u>. Divine]   <u>Spadone</u> divine
27. a'! So]   a, so
29. midwife. All]   midwife, all
30. mouth;]   mouth,
31. head to]   head, to
    Posset. ----]   Posset----
32. right?]   right,
33. thou]   thon
34. right.]   right,
36. which, Sirrah]   which Sirrah
40. snapper./ Twit]   snapper, twit
41. pendants./ Though]   pendants, though
46. all. Make]   all, make
    man!]   man,
53. belly! The]   belly, the
54. used.]   used,
55. castingbottle]   casting-/ bottle
58. bason./ Make]   bason, make
60. Hold! take]   Hold take
    Duccat. As]   Duccat, as
61. cloathes--]   cloathes.
63. Yes, or]   Yes or
    ones.]   ones,
65. againe. Reputation]   againe, reputation
74. married--]   married.
84. advantage./]   advantage,/
91. sirrah? Ha?]   sirrah ha.
94. legs./ Eate]   legs, eate
96. downe]   dowue
    doe. There's]   doe, there's
100. on. Say]   on, say
102. man. Once]   man, once

104. Secco, away]   Secco away
     away! My]   away, my
     cals./ A']   cals, a'
105. has]   ha's
     fellowes./ A]   fellowes, a
107. Nitido. Spadone]   Nitido, Spadone
 03. Exit Secco.]   Exit.
109. young]   youug
     intelligencer? What]   intelligencer,/what
111. crimpe. 'Tis]   crimpe, 'tis
116. gelder!]   gelder?
119. rascall. Th'art]   rascall, th'art
121. mortality. Goe]   mortality, goe
122. Nuns! Sing]   Nuns sing
123. song. All]   song, all
     get'st]   ge'tst
125. Midwives. Farewell]   Midwives, farewell
127. well! If]   well, if
128. this (crackrope) let]   this crack-/rope) let
129. cole-sacke.]   cole-sacke,
     yee ( ]   yee, (
131. Nit. [Sings] And]   Nit. And . . . doe. sing.
 04. Exit Nitido and Spadone.]   Exeunt.

[I. iii]

  1. me./]   me,/
  2. resolution. As]   resolution, as
 10. Why, Castamela]   Why Castamela
 13. equall. Now]   equall: now
 15. gulf]GD   guilt
 17. plenty. 'Tis]   plenty, 'tis
 19. to.]   to,

21. prosperity. I]   prosperity, I
26. lends]GD   lend
28. Oh]   oh
29. desires. The]   desires, the
    has]   ha's
30. pride/]   pride,/
33. sence/]   sence,/
35. luxurie/ Of]   luxurie of
41. wanton.]   wanton:
42. too--]   too,
47. yee. You]   yee, you
50. welfare. 'Tis]   welfare, 'tis
51. observed. Possesse]   observed, possesse
52. me. Let]   me, let
54. of]   off
55. mortality. The]   mortality, the
58. and]   aud
    and am receiv'd]   aud receiv'd
    receiv'd. Observe]   receiv'd, observe
    sister--]   sister,
63. up/]   up,/
65. wants;/]   wants/
70. advancement--]   advancement,
71. little,/]   little./
72. burthen. But]   burthen, but
74. maintenance. Why]   maintenance, why
75. mysterie/]   mysterie?/
77. Conceal'd till]   Conceal'd, till
    it./]   it,/
80. cheating-]   cheating;
    unthrifts/]   unthrifts,/
81. at;]   at:
83. City-]   City,

       lies;]   lies:
 86. reputation-]   reputation,
 89. nakednesse-]   nakednesse:
 92. lodging. These]   lodging: these
 94. experience/]   experience,/
 96. has]   ha's
102. hope, for]   hope for
103. supportance./]   supportance,/
106. amazement/]   amazement;/
107. So]   <u>S</u>o
109. unrefin'd. Then]   unrefin'd, then
110. price./]   price,/
114. satisfaction. If]   satisfaction: if
122. open'd/]   open'd,/
129. freedome. We]   freedome, we
130. fortunes. Henceforth]   fortunes henceforth
134. t'ee. I]   t'ee, I
135. Ladyes?/]   Ladyes,/
137. beauties is]   beauties, is
138. time. Th'are]   time, th'are
139. <u>Castamela</u>, chast]   <u>Castamela</u> chast
       chast! I]   chast, I
142. so]GD   to
       words/]   words,/
144. counsaile. But]   counsaile, but
 03. Clarella]   ClarelIa
147. of. -- Sweetest]   of--sweetest
149. respects. <u>Deare</u>]   respects: <u>Deare</u>
151. Society/]   Society,/
160. deny'd./]   deny'd:/
161. shall. [Aside] Now]   shall, now
 04. Exit.]   Q. has no stage direction here.
163. Brother, one]   Brother one

        anon./]   anon/
164. We]   we
169. coach./]   coach,/
        hence,/]   hence./
 05. Exit all but Romanello.]   Exeunt.
174. Amongst]   amongst
176. changes. I]   changes, I
        resolute/]   resolute,/
 06. Exit.]   Exeunt.

[II. i]

  2. meane. Unkind]   meane, unkind
        past/]   past,/
  4. company. Was]   company, was
  6. and]   aud
        place ought]   place, ought
  7. duties/]   duties,/
 13. pitty,]   pitty)
        us) how]   us! how
 15. certaine/]   certaine,/
 16. courtiers would]   courtiers, would
 17. viands-]   viand:
 20. Court. Full]   Court: full
 22. honours now]   honours, now
 23. me. But]   me, but
 24. tis. The]   tis, the
 29. so./]   so:/
 31. obedience. Fie]   obedience, fie
        Fie, methinks]   fie methinks
 32. pettish,]   pettish;
 33. toysome. 'Tis]   toysome, 'tis
 37. ringings./]   ringings/

40. Rudenesse!/]   rudenesse/
41. shal!--]   shal--
    Sawcy]   sawcy
    manners!/]   manners,/
42. stay./]   stay,/
44. name-]   name,
    Lady./]   Lady;/
48. Madam.--]   Madam--
    Marke]   marke
49. Sure]   sure
55. cal him]   calhim
    too. Why]   too, why
56. has]   ha's
57. strange. Oh]   strange, oh
59. man chang'd]   man) chang'd
    woman)/]   woman,/
60. this. She]   this, she
    A']   'A
    stands/ Just]   stands just
64. has]   ha's
    yee./]   yee:
65. hand, insooth]   hand insooth
72. defie-]   defie,
76. roundly. Doe's]   roundly, doe's
78. awhile. This]   awhile; this
79. Both. As]   Ambo. As
03. Exit Camillo and Vespuci.]   Exeunt.
80. Fabricio- Oh]   Fabricio, oh
    cruell-/]   cruell;/
81. justifie/]   justifie,/
85. unbroken. No]   unbroken, no
86. gifts]WGD   guifts
89. thoughts to]   thoughts, to

91. rumor is]   rumor, is
    enough to]   enough, to
92. actions. 'Twas]   actions, 'twas
102. worst, desire]   worst desire
104. wives-]   wives:
    innocence,/]   innocence/
105. onely./]   onely,/
106. Fabricio]WGD   Fabritio
108. losse. Without]   losse; without
111. separation. Wherein]   separation, wherein
113. So]   so
120. now. But]   now, but
122. th']   'th
123. Fabricio]WGD   Fabritio
125. foole to]   foole, to
126. carriage./]   carriage:/
129. better. 'Twere]   better: 'twere
131. doo't./]   doo't,/
132. Doo't, excellentest]   Doo't excellentest
136. commerce./]   commerce,
137. supplies. Mean]   supplies, mean
138. t'ee. I]   t'ee, I
140. neere? Vespuci.]   neere, Vespuci.
143. heart. --Kisse]   heart--kisse
    me. Nay]   me, nay
144. swoon. --Y'ave]WGD   sown--y'ave
145. too. ----Beshrew]WGD   to----beshrew
146. blessing. --[To Cam. and Ves.] Turne]   blessing
                                                  --turne
    banquerout/ Out]   banque-/ rout out
147. dores! --Sirrah]   dores--sirrah
    whipt,/]   whipt./
 05. Exit Fabricio.]   Exit Fa.

149. ist]   i'st
150. here. I]   here: I
152. petition-/]   petition,/
154. needs. A]   needs, a
161. now. Sha'not]   now: shanot
162. stands. Sure]   stands, sure
163. yee./]   yee:/
164. There]   there
166. certainely./]   certainely,/
167. pleasure!/]   pleasure:/
168. thee. In]   thee, in
170. deare./]   deare:/
 06. All Exit.]   Exeunt.

[II. ii]

 1. Thou]   thou
 3. home, art]   home art
 4. qualmes. No]   qualmes, no
 5. see./]   see:/
 6. (man)? Be]   (man) be
 7. no! Heere's]   no, heere's
 8. place. 'Tis]   place 'tis
10. puzzles onely]   puzzles, onely
    bare]   barre
    it./]   it,/
11. plate]GD   place
    Soft]   soft
13. Neate]   neate
15. Satiety]WGD   Saciety
    waterworkes?/]   waterworkes,/
16. eyes/]   eyes,/
19. Fancie/]   Fancie,/

20. abstracted. Noe]   abstracted: noe
24. <u>Troylo</u>! Were]   <u>Troylo</u>: were
27. possible/]   possible,/
33. discovery./]   discovery;/
39. infirme by]   infirme, by
40. Gallies,/]   Gallies/
41. faculty/]   faculty,/
43. Sex must]   Sex, must
    distinguish;/]   distinguish:/
48. spirit,/]   spirit;/
52. minde. A]   minde, a
53. all. To]   all; to
54. threatning,]   threatniug:
58. <u>Troylo</u>!]   <u>Troylo</u>,
62. sillable./]   sillable,/
63. admirable! 'Tis]   admirable, 'tis
    so. --Pish]   so--pish
    it!]   it,/
64. a']   'a
65. may./]   may,/
68. flame;]   flame:
69. too./]   too;/
76. trayne,/]   trayne;/
78. such/]   such,/
80. decency/]   decency,/
81. envy;]   envy,
83. ignorance. The]   ignorance: the
88. Yellowes?]   Yellowes.
91. guardianesse. It]   guardianesse, it
96. little/]   little,/
99. musicians]   musicke
101. city./]   city,/
102. that./]   that;/

104. farthest,]   farthest;
     wedding. Wherfore]   wedding, wherfore
113. insufficiency. And]   insufficiency, and
116. taken. ----]   taken----
     Sister]   sister
120. shortly/]   shortly./
121. fuller. --]   fuller--
124. exquisite. I]   exquisite, I
125. creatures. These]   creatures;/ These
126. solemnity are]   solemnity, are
     uncommon. My]   uncommon; my
128. bounties. Shals]   bounties, shals
131. stand. Bill]   stand, Bill
     doe. Thou'st]   doe; thou'st
132. Honey. Wee'l]   Honey, wee'l
134. it. And]   it, and
139. wombe! ----]   wombe----
140. has]   ha's
141. whole./ For]   whole: for
143. carriage-/ from]   carriage; from
148. shey?/]   shey,/
153. Spadone./ Nay]   Spadone, nay
154. th'ast]   tha'st
158. wedding,/ Free]   wedding, free
160. thoughts now]   thoughts, now
     now, Lady]   now Lady
161. Castamela! fie]   Castamela fie
     fie!/]   fie,/
162. All.]   Om.
163. any]   a y
     meanes! The]   meanes, the
164. excus'd/]   excus'd,/
166. time. Grant]   time, grant

on./ <u>Troy</u>. Command]GD   on./ Command
167. Lady.----Every]   Lady,----every
168. Partner. --Nay]   Partner--nay
     <u>Spadone</u> must]   <u>Spadone</u>, must
169. heart./ I'me]   heart, I!me
170. heaviest in]   heaviest/ In
     company./ <u>Troy</u>. Strike]   company./ Strike
 04. <u>Dance</u>./ So]   <u>Dance</u>./ <u>Troy</u>. So
172. motion. On]   motion: on
173. nimbly./]   nimbly,/
175. so. Yet]   so, yet
177. sirrah?/]   sirrah./
179. forsooth. You]   forsooth; you
180. owne. You]   owne,/ you
181. rubs. 'Tis]   rubs; 'tis
187. now. Ile]   now, Ile
193. day. ---I]   day,---I
195. nothing! I]   nothing, I
196. purpose. Whoreson]   purpose, whoreson
199. businesse. <u>Buts</u>]   businesse, <u>Buts</u>
203. Oh]   oh
 06. Exit Spadone.]   <u>Exit</u>.
205. Sweeting. ----Your]   Sweeting, ----your
206. Gentlemen. To]   Gentlemen; to
     virgins./]   virgins;/
207. care./]   care,/
208. away. ----Sweet]   away----sweet
209. returne. [Aside] Now]   returne, 'now
 07. Exit all but Mor. and Cas.]   Q. has no stage di-
                                          rection here.
210. Ladiship./ I]   Ladiship. I
211. shal not]   shal/ Not
     long./_____]   long./ <u>Ex</u>. severally <u>Morosa</u> staies

<u>Castamela.</u>

212. Who]   who
     has]   ha's
216. him./]   him:/
     Whom]   whom
219. Feele]   feele
220. hands-]   hands,
224. eye. Should]   eye; should
226. degrees,/]   degrees;/
230. <u>one</u>./]   <u>one</u>,/
233. then/(Religious]   then/Religious
236. tormentor. Let's]   tormentor; let's
238. scandall. (Rare]   scandall (rare
239. You]   you
     Lordship-/]   Lordship,/
241. <u>one</u>)-/]   <u>one</u>)/
242. conceit. Hee's]   conceit: Hee's
246. power,]   power:
248. Cannot? Prethee]   Cannot, prethee
249. plainer. I]   plainer: I
257. else.--[Aside] She]   else--she
     cunning. --Looke]   cunning--looke
259. palme. --/ Umh]   palme--umh
260. Rellish]   rellish
     There]   there
261. it. What]   it, what
262. all. Goe]   all, goe
     tutoring;/]   tutoring,
263. scholar. Ile]   scholar, Ile
264. not. But]   not, but
267. familie. Your]   familie, your
     brother]WGD   master
     him/]   him,/

268. him/]   him,/
269. horse. In]   horse, in
272. welcome. I'st]   welcome, i'st
273. Ladiship;/]   Ladiship,/
275. that?/]   that./
281. principall! I]   principall, I
288. throwne;]   throwne,
     minion./]   minion,/
  08. Exit Morosa and Castamela.]   Exeunt.

[III. i]

   7. reaches. --I]   reaches--I
   9. ruin'd-]   ruin'd;
  12. part. ----]   part-----
  15. fashion'd/ The]   fashion'd the
  19. this,/]   this;/
  22. done/ All]   done all
  24. practises;]   practises:
  26. 'em]   em
  27. up. What]   up, what
  28. Let]   let
     remove]WGD   romove
  37. for't]   fort
  38. shape.]   shape,
     You know]GD   and know
  44. quack]GD   quaik
  49. owne./]   owne,/
  53. laughter./]   laughter:/
  62. action. 'Twill]   action: 'twill
  67. me,/]   me/
  69. event/]   event,/
  72. yet]   it

Queres?]   Queres,?
73. silent! Else]   silent, else
74. earnest. What]   earnest, what
    Fie!/]   fie;/
76. provided. Aske]   provided, aske
03. Exit Romanello.]   Exit.
78. Seignior./]   Seignior;/
80. income. ----]WGD incombe-----
    Love]   love
83. trustie./]   trustie,/
86. Man]   man
88. a' does]   'adoes
89. delight./]   delight:/
93. a']   'a
94. not;/]   not:/
96. case. 'Las]   case, 'las
100. about. He]   about: he
    haste, beleeve]   haste beleeve
05. Exit Troylo and Nitido.]   Exit.

[III. ii]

2. indeed. I]   indeed; I
10. doe. I]   doe I
    forehead;/]   forehead,/
17. Thou]   thou
18. replid'st: Because]   replid'st, because
    Soveraigne,/]   Soveraigne/
21. Hereat]   hereat
22. wink'd;]   wink'd,
    stard'st./]   stard'st/
23. observ't. Be]   observ't, be
24. thee. In]   thee: in

26. complement. Ah]   complement: ah
31. But]   but
    sociable./]   sociable;/
34. share-]   share;
35. 'tis. Since]   'tis, since
36. Camillo, I]   Camillo I
43. t'other]WD   tother
45. then,/]   then;/
51. addition:/]   addition/
54. all true]   all! true
    honour,/]   honour;/
57. soule. --He]   soule--he
58. servant./]   servant;/
59. readily. On]   readily on
    t'other]GD   tother
61. it./ So]   it, so
02. Fabricio]WGD   Fabritio
70. us. Oh]   us; oh
74. Ladies. --They'le]   Ladies--they'le
75. that!/]   that,/
79. ever./]   ever:/
81. 'Tis]   T'is
84. mention fals]   mention/Fals
85. bounty. I]   bounty, I
87. world? Where's]   world, where's
    Good]   good
03. Exit Fabricio.]   Exit.
97. sweetest,/]   sweetest/
98. eare. ----Beshrew't]   eare ----beshrew't
99. eye. --]   eye--
101. off,/]   off;/
102. off. Forbeare]   off, forbeare
103. eye./]   eye,/

106. Gentlemen./Speak]   Gentlemen: speak
 04. Exit Camillo and Vespuci.]   Ex. Ca. Ve.
111. me-]   me,
113. husbands. 'Tis]   husbands: 'tis
115. merriments;/]   merriments,/
116. enjoy-]   enjoy;
120. would'st./]   would'st/
123. humour./]   humour:/
128. distance,/]   distance;/
129. away;]   away,
130. attempt]GD   attempted
133. me. Not]   me; not
135. hear't. ----Oh]   hear't,----oh
136. angrie. 'Las]   angrie; 'las
137. A']   A
     mind,]   mind:
138. little;]   little,
139. quiet./]   quiet;/
144. thou'lt]WD   thoul't
 05. Exit Flavia and Julio.]   Exit.

[III. iii]

  2. gamballs. A']   gamballs, a
     does a']   does a
  3. O]   ò
  5. clack./A']   clack: a
  7. Rabets-]   Rabets;
     there! Your]   there, your
  8. Madona,]   Madona;
     a'has]   a has
     too. There's]   too:/There's
  9. dunce else]   dunce, else

        else. I]   else I
11. me. I]   me, I
13. That]   that
15. Signior]   signior
16. doore. Some]   doore; some
17. Wife. I]   Wife, I
19. case-]   case,
21. a']   a
    Rather]   rather
22. first. I]   first I
24. Page. Let]   Page;/ let
    forehead. Ha]   forehead, ha
25. ye;]   ye,
30. tips. You]   tips/you
    yet./ Have]   yet: have
31. man. A]   man, a
    a' be]   a be
32. might/ not know]   might know
36. Hee's]   hee's
37. yet; he]   yet, he
39. Nay, she]   Nay she
40. thousand,]   thousand;
41. Spadone. I]   Spadone, I
42. passion;]   passion,
44. ridiculous!----Look]   ridiculous,--look
46. newcome]   new-/come
48. him-/selfe. But]   himselfe: but
50. Page-]   Page;
51. heart-]   heart:
52. bottome?/]   bottome./
53. matter-]   matter,
54. I. Be]   I, be
    patient. You'l]   patient you'l

02. Clarella, Silvia]   Clarella Silvia
66. beauties./]   beauties,/
67. faire. Forsooth]   faire forsooth
68. such. Monsters]   such, Monsters
74. love, fine]   love fine
80. else. It]   else it
81. pleasure, travaile]   pleasure travaile
    travaile;]   travaile,
83. rope. Oh]   rope: oh
86. lies, I]   lies I
    sweare, abominably]   sweare abominably
88. Inhumanly!----[Pinches Mor.] Keepe]   Inhumanly,
                                                   ----Keepe
89. earnest./ You]   eannest: /You
90. hard. Go]   hard, go
92. hornes. There's]   hornes, there's
95. that! The]   that, the
106. found./]   found/
107. vanities:/]   vanities;/
108. babler;/]   babler:/
109. Tawny?]   Tawny,
     wounded;/]   wounded./
110. Ribbands? she's]   Ribbands she's
     forsaken;/]   forsaken?/
112. unbroken;/]   unbroken:/
113. 'em]   em
114. famine./]   famine:/
116. Not]   not
     females!/]   females?
119. forsooth. Should]   forsooth, should
120. foole,]   foole;
122. two-]   two;
123. thee! Am]   thee; am

125. devices. Now]   devices, now
126. stripling. Thou]   stripling, thou
128. for't. Take]   fort, take
    comfort:/]   comfort,/
129. gummes;/]   gummes:/
131. Fortune./]   Fortune./
135. a' rub'd]   a rub'd
    forehead. 'Twas]   forehead, 'twas
137. him! Let]   him, let
138. mine./]   mine,/
 03. Exit Secco.]   <u>Exit</u> <u>Secco</u> <u>and</u> <u>Spadone</u>.
 04. Exit Spadone.]   _____
146. not, <u>I</u>]   not <u>I</u>
    <u>I</u>./]   <u>I</u>,/
148. Sir? <u>I</u>]   Sir, <u>I</u>
 05. Exit Morosa.]   <u>Exit</u>.
153. A']   A
    ne're]   nere
 06. Enter]   <u>Enters</u>
155. Why, you]   Why you
157. us./]   us,/
 07. Exit Troylo and Romanello.]WGD   _____
161. service./]   service:/
165. it. Y'ave]   it, y'ave
170. for./]   for:/
172 any/]   any;/
173. custome./]   custome,/
180. Musicke?/]   Musicke./
185. Sister;]   Sister,
011. Exit all but Octavio and Castamela.]   <u>Exit</u>. <u>Manet</u>
                                                  Octa. <u>and</u>
                                                  <u>Castamela</u>.
190. proficience. Pray]   proficience, pray

194. Law. I]   Law: I
     t'ee]   tee
197. wakings/]   wakings;/
199. so./]   so,/
206. passion. Tho]   passion, tho
208. Girle,]   Girle:
210. 'em,/]   em;/
211. can withhold]   can, withhold
     withhold. This]   withhold this
     Academy/]   Academy./
214. Virgins;]   Virgins,
216. onely-/]   onely/
217. No worse]   No, worse
     imagine./]   imagine;/
219. wickednesse your]   wickednesse, your
220. mercies./]   mercies,/
221. misery./]   misery;/
222. Beare]   beare
227. a']   a
231. bondage!/]   bondage;/
236. time;]   time:
237. this? Come]   this, come
     soberly./]   soberly,/
238. Musique./]   Musique;/
241. scandall. You]   scandall, you
242. meanes, a]   meanes. A
243. wants. Convert]   wants, convert
244. Court; let]   Court: let
248. worthie,/]   worthie;/
250. Chronicle./]   Chronicle:/
251. piety;]   piety:
252. stone,]   stone;
260. what.----]   what----
261. w'ee]   we'e

263. perfect]   prefect
     here./]   here/
013. All Exit.]   Exeunt omnes.

[IV. i]

  5. D'ee]   Dee
  6. Office./]   Office:/
 14. Why]   why
 15. Lady,/]   Lady/
 18. sweetnes,/]   sweetnes:/
 19. Gallantry./]   Gallantry/
 20. o'th']   oth'
 23. sport./ You]   sport, you
 26. 'em,]   em:
 27. withold.----]   withold----
     not./]   not,/
 28. bargaine;]   bargaine,
 29. now;/]   now,/
 31. Traytor.]   Traytor:
 32. flourish,/]   flourish./
 34. patience,/]   patience:/
 39. Livio;]   Livio,
     it./]   it,/
 40. projects./]   projects:/
 43. You]   you
 47. contempt,]   contempt:
 49. Sir./]   Sir,/
 50. Signior./]   Signior,/
 52. Devotion./]   Devotion:/
 53. me.]   me,
 54. cannot. For]   cannot for
     past,]   past;

55. me./]   me:/
57. Foole]   foole
60. <u>Castamela</u>, Sister]   <u>Castamela</u> Sister
63. confidence,]   confidence;
65. Thy]   thy
69. blood,]   blood;
74. thee./]   thee:/
75. manners!/]   manners:/
77. desires. 'Tis]   desires: 'tis
78. now./]   now:/
86. follow. Here]   follow, here
    issue./]   issue:/
89. gallant,/]   gallant/
99. a']   a
102. broken!/]   broken,/
104. Young]   young
02. Exit Livio.]   <u>Exit.</u>
107. nature,/]   nature;/
109. noble-]   noble,
    credulous my]   credulous, my
111. Ne're]   Nere
112. runs. But]   runs: but
114. mad.]   mad,
115. breech.]   breech:
119. Ladies, good]   Ladies good
122. What]   what
131. faces. His]   faces: his
133. for't.]   for't:
    <u>Whiskin</u>, untrusse]   <u>Whiskin</u> untrusse
134. moyle-]   moyle;
135. next. The Horns]GD   next, avaunt thy turn comes
                         next; avaunt the Horns
136. advanced! Hence]   advanced; hence

137. soundly. Let]   soundly, let
140. heart./ If]   heart, if
144. Beare!/ Fa]   Beare, fa
145. fa! To't]   fa; to't
     To't, to't]   to't, to't
149. and]   &
150. Scould, Coxcombe]   Scould Coxcombe
155. now.]   now:
157. outrage./]   outrage:/
159. Quickly]   quickly
160. choller. What's]   choller; what's
161. Humh, how's]   Humh how's
     How's]   how's
     Is]   is
163. dwindle. ----]   dwindle,----
166. people, Jewes]   people/ Jewes
170. beast,]   beast:
171. beast, in]   beast in
     Cuckold./ Nay]   Cuckold: nay
174. so. But]   so: but
176. Morosa. You]   Morosa, you
178. 'em. This]   em: this
180. Infant!]   Infant;
183. Spadone. My]   Spadone, my
184. grosse. Truth]   grosse: truth
185. Speake]   speake
187. speake? Alas]   speake, alas
     speake,/I]   speake I
190. Damne]   Dambe
     Pipe./ Where]   Pipe: where
192. baby, must]WGD baby must
194. I am an]   I an
203. 'em]   em
204. Doing]   doing

212. abus'd. They]   abus'd, they
     scorne, jeere]   scorne jeere
214. Pander; the]   Pander̃/the
217. <u>Secco</u>, for]   <u>Secco</u> for
218. Woman, <u>I</u>]   Woman; <u>I</u>
220. wot. That's]   wot, that's
224. Law]   law
 04. Exit Secco.]   <u>Exit.</u>
229. has]   ha's
231. art. The]   art; the
235. child! There]   child; there
238. a']W   a
240. noveltie./]   noveltie,/
241. reconcil'd.]   reconcil'd,
     <u>Spadone</u>,/]   <u>Spadone</u>;/
242. e're]   ere
245. love./]   love,/
 05. Exit all but Spadone and Nitido.] <u>Ex. Troy. La.</u>
247. youngling. Have]   youngling: have
248. Thanke]   thanke
     for't./]   for't/
251 possible! Give]   possible, give
252. fist. We]   fist, we
     henceforth;]   henceforth,
255. forth. Come]   forth: Come
 06. Exit Spadone and Nitido.]   <u>Exeunt.</u>

[IV. ii]

  5. there./]   there:/
  6. late. You]   late, you
  8. entertainments./]   entertainments,/
  9. Collations,/]   Collations;/

12. open./]   open/
16. Familie,]   Familie;
19. discourses;---]   discourses---
22. with./]   with;/
26. patient./]   patient:/
27. repine not]   not repine
29. liberty./]   liberty:/
31. sence,/ Vespuci]   sence, Vespuci
32. observe./]   observe,/
33. ye-]   ye,
35.)-are]   )are
40. ne're]   nere
52. Marriage,/]   Marriage:
60. afterwards,/]   afterwards/
62. Condition,/]   Condition;/
66. pursuit. T'acquaint]   pursuit; t'acquaint
67. living./]   living:/
74. are./]   are:/
80. example. When]   example: when
84. ratified.--My]   ratified,--my
87. distrust. Reigne]   distrust: reigne
89. union.]   union,
92. love. [Takes her hand] You]   love, you
94. me. Noblest]   me; noblest
99. it-]   it;
102. linke]   liuke
104. commends, by]   commends by
      deputation,/]   deputation/
106. liberally,/Above]   liberally, above
113. consider/]   consider,/
115. affection,]   affection;
116. circumstance,/ Proceed]   circumstance, proceed
123. youth. She]   youth; she

owne./]   owne,/

129. in. Some]   in, some

133. his.----You]   his----you

134. advantages. It]   advantages, it

     state./]   state:/

142. courted./]   courted,/

147. maintenance. Livio's]   maintenance; Livios

148. purchase./]   purchase,/

149. Sir. Send]   Sir, send

     on't./]   on't;/

151. Full----]   Full,----

     made]   mate

     already./]   already,/

155. coldnes. There]   coldnes, there

159. tales. Troth]   tales; troth

160. Riddles./]   Riddles,/

163. Master;/]   Master:/

171. Shee's]   Shees

174. Choyce./]   Choyce,/

175.), more]   ) more

179. Pretty swiftly./]   Pretty swiftly;/

183. noe, once]   noe once

     ever.----This]   ever;----this

184. second.----]   second;----

185. it. Scan]   it; scan

186. plainnesse;]   plainnesse,

189. parting.]   parting;

 05. Exit Livio.]   Exit.

195. resolv'd. Upon]   resolv'd; upon

196. grounded./]   grounded:/

197. home. Lost]   home, lost

 06. Exit Romanello and Flavia.]   Exeunt.

[V. i]

2. abroad, nor]   abroad,/Nor
8. honour. We]   honour, we
13. o're]   ore
16. household.]   hoshould;
18. uprores, bandie]   uprores, (bandie
    noise amongst]   noise) amongst
19. madnesse;]   madnesse,
20. punishment. A]   punishment; a
22. favor. Since]   favor, since
27. cole. Take]   cole; take
28. beautie,]   beautie;
30. neighbours,/]   neighbours;/
31. ye. Now]   ye; now
33. worme. Pray]   worme, pray
34. Me]   me
35. out. On]   out; on
36. knees. I]   knees, I
38. forgivenes./]   forgivenes,/
39. her./]   her,/
40. kindnes.]   kindnes:
41. word. Ile]   word; Ile
    madnes./]   madnes,/
43. Ladies.]   Ladies,
02. Exit Secco and Nitido.]   Exeunt.
53. Familie,/]   Familie/
58. contrivements,/]   contrivements./
67. receiv'd.]   receiv'd;
69. talke. ----She]   talke ----she
70. him?/]   him./
78. truth.]   truth:
84. manners./ Know]   manners; know

92. blood?/]   blood;/
95. borne. For]   borne: for
97. thus.--if]   thus;--if
04. Exit Octavio.]   Exit.
100. Livio! Wherefore]   Livio, wherefore
103. Romanello. He]   Romanello, he
106. Academie./]   Academie:/
108. Father. Talkes]   Father, talkes
     on't]   ont
111. sufferance! Canst]   sufferance, canst
112. 'Twas]   'twas
114. That her]   That, her
119. Livio?]   Livio.
120. say. Your]   say; your
122. there's]   theres
     remedy;/]   remedy,/
128. grounds. This]   grounds, this
129. promise, ere]   promise ere
132. The]   the
     short./]   short,/
133. houre, you]   houre: you
     vow?/]   vow./
134. to./]   to,/
136. Julio,/]   Iulio/
138. busines./]   busines,/
141. ye]WD   y'e
143. strange. Is't]   strange, is't
     possible?]   possible.
05. Exit Troylo and Livio.]   Exeunt.

[V. ii]

1. story;/]   story,/

2. to th']   toth'

6. truth. O]   truth; O

    o're]   ore

10. education./]   education:/

24. roofe that's]   roofe, that's

25. are./]   are;/

29. providence. For]   providence for

30. power.----Our]   power,----our

33. noble. We]   noble, we

41. live./]   live:/

47. by't. Heartily]   by't, heartily

51. mercy.--Was't]   mercy;--was't

52. Bee]   bee

54. merry.--/Hast]   merry,--hast

56. toward. Pray]   toward, pray

58. neatly]   featly

61. can. Time]   can, time

62. to't. Young]   to't; young

63. Fie]   fie

64. hand. Husband]   hand; hisband

    husband like]   hisband, like

66. Shall]   shall

69. keep'st.]   keep'st,

70. time. Honest]   time, honest

72. drawer;]   drawer,

76. boy. Sit]   boy,/sit

86. wits, I]   wits I

87. No]   no

98. eyes. The]   eyes, the

104. Well]   well

105. too. (Prethee]   too (prethee

    roughly.)]   roughly)

106. And]   and

```
        o'th']      oth'
        What]       what
112. by. Most]         by, most
114. it. 'Tis]         it, 'tis
121. ne're]         nere
122. cheate.----This]               cheate;----this
130. muske!/ What]      muske, what
132. Set]       set
136. that. Dispatch]       that; dispatch
139. man;]       man,
143. keene. It]      keene, it
146. Signior.----When]       Signior,----when
147. Tell]       tell
149. Hang]       hang
156. gullet.----You]       gullet;/----you
158. truth. (Move]       truth, (move
159. side]       file
        side.) Out]       file) out
160. leap?/]       leap./
162. pickle. Have]       pickle, have
        canst./]       canst,
167. This]       this
169. asse!]       asse,
172. thee. This]       thee: this
177. angry! Feele]       angry, feele
181. yellowes!/ Have]       yellowes: have
187. on't. Deare]       on't; deare
188. discretion. Nitido]       discretion: Nitido
        too./ No]       too; no
 06. All Exit.]       Exit.
```

[V. iii]

```
  6. parley. Night]       parley; night
```

```
 9. rack. Here]      rack; here
11. had. Pray]       had; pray
13. tongue/ From]       tongue from
14. untruths.]       untruths,
15. now]WGD  ow
    mee!/]WGD  eem,/
16. This]      this
25 'em]     em
37. lively./]       lively,/
39. life.----]       life;-----
03. Exit Troylo.]       Exit.
40. e're]     ere
44. lapidarie./]       lapidarie;/
47. they? They]       they, they
52. me./]     me,/
54. Bonony./]       Bonony/
38. unpleasant./]       unpleasant,/
65. lewdnesse]       leudnesse
66. riot.]      riot;
69. heaven;]       heaven,
    him./]     him;/
72. word. These]       word, these
74. friends. Examine]       friends; examine
    lustre./]       lustre/
75. Wherfore]       wherfore
76. me./]      me,/
80. once. What]       once, what
81. one./]     one,/
83. past;]      past,
85. blanke. Excuse]       blanke, excuse
87. Castamela?/]       Castamela,/
92. Brother]       Brorher
94. secresie;]       secrecie,
```

103. knowledge;]   knowledge,
104. prospered. He's]   prospered, he's
107. these,/]   these/
109. Sister;]   Sister,
110. World. Indeed]   World; indeed
111. are.]   are,
     other. How]   other; how
112. speake. Now]   speake; now
115. fortune. If]   fortune, if
116. them; here]   them, here
117. henceforth. Only]   henceforth; only
131. Clowne./]   Clowne:/
133. perform'd. Henceforth]   perform'd henceforth
134. title.]   title:

APPENDIX C

HISTORICAL COLLATION

[Prologue]

   4. ·eare]Q   care]W   ear]GD
  16. your own]   your even]Q   your even]W   your own]GD

[I. i]

  30. Th']QWD   The]G
      o're]Q   o'er]WGD
      Ligorne]Q   Leghorn]WG   Ligorne]D
  38. Angentorato]Q   Argentorato]GD   Angentorato]W
  39. Whiles]QD   Whilst]WG
  42. Y'are]Q   You're]WD   You are]G
  02. Octavio, and Nitido.]   Octavo, and Nitido.]Q
          Octavio and Nitido.]W   Octavio.]GD
  88. intrust]QD   entrust]WG
  94. Sir/Owes]Q   sir,/ Owes]GD   Weber feels a line has
                                     been lost between "Sir"
                                     and "Owes." Accord-
                                     ingly, he at this point
                                     includes an ellipsis
                                     in his text.
  03. Exit Octavio and Nitido.]   Exit. Oct. Page.]Q
          Exeunt Oct. and Nit.]W   Exit.]GD
 109. cup]QWG   cap]D
 110. their]QW   that]GD

```
     need]QW    nod]GD
121. yee]Q    you]WG    ye]D
127. Batchelor. -- Lord, so,]   Batchelor -- Lord, so,]Q
     bachelor? -- Lord, so?]W    bachelor lord?
     -- so!]GD
128. respect of]QWD   respect to]G
131. thy]GD    my]QW
132. we will]QGD    we shall]W
```

[I. ii]

```
 32. yee]Q    you]WG    ye]D
 41. decrements]QWG    decrement]D
 71. yee]Q    you]WG    ye]D
 72. wholesome of]Q    wholesome [yoke] of]WGD
 83. sweetnes]Q    sweets]W    sweetness]GD
 88. should]QWD    shall]G
 89. yee]Q    ye]WD    you]G
105. A']    a']QW    he]GD
108. moyle]Q    moil]WD    mule]G
```

[I. iii]

```
  8. conster]Q    construe]WGD
 15. gulf]GD    guilt]QW
 23. yee]Q    you]WG    ye]D
 26. lends]GD    lend]QW
 29. yee]Q    you]WG    ye]D
 32. Whiles]QD    Whilst]WG
     yee]Q    you]WG    ye]D
 47. yee]Q    you]WG    ye]D
 02. fresh suited]    fresh suited]QW    richly habited]GD
 58. and am receiv'd.]    aud receiv'd]Q    am received]W
```

         and received]G   and receiv'd]D
  72. As single]QW   A single]GD
      burthen]QD   burden]WG
 142. so the]GD   to the]WQ
 164. instruct at]QWD   instruct you at]G
 167. Whether]QW   Whither]GD

[II.i]

  10. travaile]Q   travel]W   travail]GD
  23. we beare]QW   we'll bear]GD   we bear]W
  27. on us]QGD   upon us]W
  52. from bankerouts]Q   from bankerupt's]W
         from a bankrupt's]GD
  56. a']Q   he]WGD
  57. were strange]QW   were [most] strange]GD
  74. yee]Q   ye]WD   you]G
  83. These]QW   Those]GD
  86. gifts]WGD   guifts]Q
 102. which feare]Q   which fear]W
         which [through] fear]GD
      worst]QW   worse]GD
 106. Fabricio]   Fabritio]Q   Fabricio]WGD
 113. Adulteresse]Q   adult'ress]W   adultress]GD
 123. Fabricio]   Fabritio]Q   Fabricio]WGD
 133. goodnesse]Q   goodness]W   sadness]GD
 138. t'ee]Q   to you]WG   t'ye]D
 144. swoon]WGD   sown]Q
 145. too]WGD   to]Q
 161. Sha'not]W   shanot]Q   shall not]GD
 167. sights were]QGD   sights are]W
      exc'lent]Q   excellent]WGD
 170. t'ee]Q   t'ye]WGD

[II. ii]

11. in plate]GD   in place]QW
15. Satiety]WGD   Saciety]Q
27. yee]Q   you]WG   ye]D
28. t'ee]Q   t'you]WG   t'ye]D
64. a']   'a]Q   he]WGD
65. a']Q   he]WGD
66. a' wod]Q   he would]WGD
109. a']Q   he]WGD
114. A']Q   He]WGD
116. I'me]Q   I'm]WD   I am]G
140. a']Q   he]WGD
     yee]Q   ye]WD   you]G
145. moyle]Q   moil]WD   mule]G
148. shey]QW   hey]GD
151. yee]Q   you]WG   ye]D
166. on./ Troy. Command]GD   on./ Command]Q
         on./ Mor. Command]W
173. Yee . . . yee]Q   You . . . you]WG   Ye . . . ye]D
187. 'em]QW   him]GD
191. a']Q   he]WGD
212. 'em]QD   them]WG
214. May it]QWG   May't]D
227. a']Q   he]GWD
232. ere]Q   e'er]WGD
248. A' . . . a']Q   He . . . he]GWD
251. A']Q   He]WGD
253. a']Q   he]WGD
     yee]Q   ye]WD   you]G
267. brother]GWD   master]Q
275. yee]Q   ye]WD   you]G

[III. i]

7. punish'd]QGD   furnish'd]W
22. Th'ast out done]Q   Thou hast done]W
        Thou hast out-done]G   Thou'st outdone]D
28. remove]WGD   romove]Q
    'em]QD   them]WG
34. Thou't]Q   Thou'lt]WGD
35. w'are]Q   we're]WD   we are]G
37. for't]   fort]Q   for it]WGD
38. You know]GD   and know]WQ
42. a']Q   he]WGD
43. a']Q   he]WGD
44. quack]GD   quaik]Q   quake]W
50. you are]QWG   you're]D
77. yee]Q   you]WG   ye]D
80. income]WGD   incombe]Q
92. supposition]QW   [im]position]G   imposition]D
93. a']   'a]Q   he]WGD
99. at's]QWD   at his]G

[III. ii]

36. is wanton]Q   is [a] wanton]WGD
43. to t'other]WD   to tother]Q   to the other]G
59. t'other]GD   tother]Q   th'other]W
02. Fabricio]WGD   Fabritio]Q
70. 'em]QD   them]Wg
72. that it is]Q   that 'tis]WG   that it's]D
    possible/ How to]QWD   possible/ To]G
77. 'Tis]QWG   It is]D
90. I, I]QD   Aye, I]W   I--I]G
96. yee]Q   you]WG   ye]D

100. ----smarts]Q   ----[It] smarts]W
          ----[it] smarts]GD
113. 'Tis]   'tis]Q   it is]WGD
130. attempt]GD   attempted]QW
132. ye]QD   you]WG
137. A']   A]Q   He]WGD
144. thou'lt]WD   thoul't]Q   you'll]G

[III. iii]

  2. A' talkes]   a/ talkes]Q   he talks]WGD
     a'/not]   a not]Q   he not]WGD
  3. O, my]   ô, my]Q   o' my]W   On my]G   O' my]D
  6. A' towzes]   a towzes]Q   he towzes]WG   he touses]D
  8. a' has]   a has]Q   he has]WGD
 31. a' be]   a be]Q   he be]WGD
 02. Romanello, like a Courtly Mountebanck]   Romanello,
        like a Courtly Mountebanck]Q   Romanello, like
        a courtly Mountebank]W   Romanello, disguised,
        as Pragnioli]G   Romanello, disguised as
        Prugnuolo]D
 65. ye]QD   you]WG
 72. treedle]QW   treddle]GD
 74. ere]Q   e'er]WGD
 98. De'e]Q   D'ye]WGD
135. a']   a]Q   he]WGD
138. finger]QD   fingers]WG
148. ye part]QWD   you part]G
153. A' ne're]   A nere]Q   He ne'er]WGD
 07. Exit Troylo and Romanello.]   Exeunt Troy. and
        Rom.]WG   Exeunt Troy. and Rom.]D
        Quarto does not contain this stage direction.
168. ye]QWD   you]G

194. t'ee]   tee]Q   t'ye]WGD
201. To aknowledge]Q   To acknowledge]WG
        T' acknowledge]D
205. belov'd]QWD   beloved]G
257. yee]Q   you]WG   ye]D
261. w'ee]   we'e]Q   wi'ye]WG   w'ye]D
263. inck'd]QG   link'd]W   nick'd]D

[IV. i]

  5. D'ee]   Dee]Q   D'ye]WGD
 42. shall stand]QD   shall be]WG
 54. past]QWG   pass'd]D
 67. falne]Q   fallen]WG   fall'n]D
 84. To expose]Q   T'expose]WGD
 89. You are]QWG   You're]D
 99. a']   a]Q   he]WGD
102. bee't]Q   be it]WGD
132. so lusty]QW   too lusty]GD
134. moyle]Q   moyl]W   mule]G   moil]D
     moyle. Avaunt, thy turn comes next. The]   moyle;
        avaunt, thy turne comes next, avaunt thy turn
        comes next; avaunt the]Q   moyl ! Avaunt! thy
        turn comes next. Avaunt! thy turn comes next.
        Avaunt! the]W   mule! avaunt! thy turn comes
        next, avaunt! the]G   moil! avaunt! thy turn
        comes next; avaunt! the]D
192. ye]QWD   you]G
194. I am an]   I an]Q   I[am] an]WGD
238. ha' led]QWD   have led]G
     a']W   a]Q   he]GD
242. how e're]   how ere]Q   howe'er]WGD
246. yee]Q   ye]WD   you]G

[IV. ii]

19. discourses]QW   discourse]GD
33. pray ye]QWD   pray you]G
40. ne're]   nere]Q   ne'er]WGD
51. forget to]QGD   presume to]W
67. T' have]QD   To have]WG
96. bold]QW   held]GD
114. yee]Q   ye]WD   you]G
121. yee]Q   ye]WD   you]G
138. I am]QG   I'm]WD
151. made]WGD   mate]Q
162. vice-gerent]Q   vicegerent]WGD
197. yee]Q   you]WG   ye]D

[V. i]

13. o're]   ore]Q   o'er]WGD
21. this is all]QGD   this all]W
31. ye simper]QWD   you simper]G
44. thee]QGD   he]W
89. You are]QWG   You're]D
119. and't]Q   an't]WGD
122. Whiles]QD   Whilst]WG
141. ye]WD   y'e]Q   you]G

[V. ii]

6. o're]   ore]Q   o'er]WGD
7. Ye . . . ye]QWD   You . . . you]G
37. Sh'as]QD   She has]WG
47. by't]QD   by it]WG
48. <u>flesh and blood</u>]Q   flesh and bone]W

            flesh and blood]GD
  52. quits]QGD   quit]W
  56. yee]Q   ye]WD   you]G
 121. ne're]   nere]Q   ne'er]WD   never]G
 155. squirting of sweet]QGD   squirting sweet]W
 157. yee]Q   ye]WD   you]G
 182. yee]Q   you]WG   ye]D

[V.iii]

  15. now]WGD   ow]Q
      mee]   eem]Q   me]WGD
  28. my Lord]Q   my love]W   my lord]GD
  36. judgements]QWG   judgement]D
      'em]QD   them]WG
  40. e're]   ere]Q   e'er]WGD
  54. Bonony]Q   Bononie]W   Bononia]G   Bonony]D
  63. whiles]QD   whilst]WG
  90. Thus when]Q   And when]W   Thus--When]GD
  95. Brother]Q   sister]W   brother]GD
 122. Prugniolo's]Q   Pragniolo's]W   Pragnioli's]G
      Prugnuolo's]D
 124. ye]QD   you]WG

APPENDIX D

CHARTS

RUNNING TITLE ANALYSIS

	Evidence	Identical Titles
Skeleton Forme I	Damaged h, F, A	$A2^V$, $B1^V$, $C4^V$, $D3^V$, $E2^V$, $E3^V$
	Damaged T, F, E & spacing	$A4^V$, $B3^V$, $C2^V$, $D1^V$, $E4^V$, $E1^V$
	Damaged A, T & spacing	A3, B4, C1, D2, E2, E3
	Damaged T, F, heavy point & spacing	A1, B2, C3, D4, E1, E4
Skeleton Forme II	Damaged A, F & spacing	A2, B1, C4, D3
	Damaged F	$A3^V$, $B4^V$, $C1^V$, $D2^V$
	Damaged T, h, F & spacing	$A1^V$, $B2^V$, $C3^V$, $D4^V$
	Damaged T, A, E	A4, B3, C2, D1
Skeleton Forme III	Damaged F, T	$F1^V$, $G1^V$, $H1^V$, $I1^V$, $K2^V$
	Conjectured	F2, G2, H2, I2, K1
	Conjectured	$F3^V$, $G3^V$, $H3^V$, $I3^V$, $K4^V$
	Conjectured	F4, G4, H4, I4, K3
Skeleton Forme IV	Damaged E & incorrect pagination of page 77 as 67	F1, G1, H3, I3, K4
	Damaged E, C	$F2^V$, $G2^V$, $H4^V$, $I4^V$, $K3^V$
	Damaged F, T	F3, G3, H1, I1, K2
	Conjectured	$F4^V$, $G4^V$, $H2^V$, $I2^V$, $K1^V$

It is, of course, apparent that there is greater evidence for the identification of skeleton formes I, II and even IV than there is for skeleton forme III. However, the consistency of the evidence that does exist makes the conjectures quite safe. Also, though the small 'T' and 'i' which are found in the titles of the second half of the play occur too frequently to be used as positive evidence, they are important in that their occurence and non-occurence are accomodated by the conjectured identifications.

SPELLING TESTS

WORD	OCCURENCE[1]
yee	A4^V, B2, B2^V, C2^V-3, C4, C4^V, D4-4, D4^V, E2, E4^V, G1, H1, H1^V, H3-3, H4^V, I2, I3, I4, K1, K1^V-2, K3^V
ye	F1, F1^V-3, F2, F3-2, F3^V, G4, G4^V, H2, I1-3, I3-2, I4-3, K4
you	D3^V, E2^V, G2-7, G2^V-2, G4, H3^V-2, H4^V-2, I1, I1^V-2, I2-3
hee	A3^V, C1, D4-2, F1^V, G3^V, G4, H4, I1^V, I2, K2^V, K3
he	A2^V-2, B2^V, C2, C4^V, D1, D3^V-3, D4^V, E2^V, E3^V, F1, F1^V, F2-2, F2^V, F3-4, F4^V, G1, G3^V, G4, H3^V-2, I1, I2-2, I2^V-2, I3^V-2, I1^V, K3^V-2
a'	B2, C2-2, D1-3, D1^V, D2-2, D3, D3^V, D4-4, E1^V-2, E2^V-2,
a	A4^V, F1-4, F1^V-3, F3, F3^V, G1, G3, H1
goe	B2, B4, C2, D3, D4, F1, I4-3, I4^V
go	F1^V, F2^V
'em	D3^V
em	F3, F4^V, K1^V

[1]The number which follows each page reference, both here and in the speech prefix chart which follows, indicates the number of times the word or prefix occurs on that page.

SPEECH PREFIXES

PREFIX	OCCURENCE
Livio	$A2^V$-2, A3
Livio.	A2, A3, $A3^V$, A4, B3, B4-2, $B4^V$
Liv.	$A2^V$, A3, A4-2, B3, $B3^V$, B4-4, C1, C4, $C4^V$-3, D1-3 $D1^V$-5, D2-2, $D3^V$, H3-4, $H3^V$-3, H4-4, $H4^V$-2, $I2^V$-3 I3-5, $K1^V$, K2-2, $K2^V$, K3-2, $K3^V$-2
Li.	$A3^V$, B3, $B3^V$, $B4^V$, $C4^V$, $F3^V$-2, F4-2, $G1^V$-5, G2-4, $G2^V$-4, G3-3, $G3^V$-2
Jul.	$C3^V$, $E4^V$-3
Ju.	E4-2
Iulio.	$E3^V$
Iul.	C4, $E4^V$, K2, $K2^V$-2, $K3^V$
Iu.	$C3^V$-3, C4, F1-3

LIST OF VARIANTS FOUND BETWEEN THE COLLATED QUARTOS[2]

PAGE	CHAPIN	BOD.#1	FOLGER	HUNTINGTON	YALE	E.C. HARVARD	B.M. #644.b.39
A1	FANCIES,	FANCIES	FANCIES	*	*	FANCIES	*
A3	H s	His	*	His	*	*	*
A3	pure,	pure	pure.	*	*	*	pure
A4	their	the r	the r	*	*	*	*
A4	beggarie	*	beggarie,	beggarie,	*	*	beggarie,
B3ᵛ	Cast.	Cast.	Cast.	Cast.	Cast.	Cast.	Cast.
B4	sister	*	*	*	*	sist er	*
B4	a. feare	a feare	a feare	a feare	*	*	a feare
C2	17	*	*	*	*	7	*
C3ᵛ	wherein	*	wherem	*	*	*	*
C4ᵛ	22	*	*	*	*	2	*
D1	him	*	*	*	h m	*	*
D3ᵛ	(May	May	May	May	May	*	May
D3ᵛ	honourable,	*	honourable;	*	*	*	*
E2	Ente	Enter	*	Enter	Enter	Enter	Enter
E3	doe,	*	*	*	*	doe	doe
E4	uth	*	Truth	Truth	*	Truth	Truth
E4ᵛ	deerest	*	*	*	deere st	deere st	deere st
F1ᵛ	from a Country	*	*	from Countrey	*	*	*

[2]An asterisk indicates when the reading of a particular quarto agrees with the Chapin copy listed in the first column.

PAGE	CHAPIN	BOD.#1	FOLGER	HUNTINGTON	YALE E.C.	HARVARD	B.M. #644.b.39
G2	the	*	*	*	e	*	*
G3^V	wee	*	ee	*	*	*	*
G4	for't:	*	*	for't.	*	*	*
I1	doe what	*	*	doe.what	*	*	*
I4^V	snip snap	*	*	*	*	snip-snap	*
K1^V	unmanly	*	*	*	*	unmanly	*
K2	now	*	xow	*	*	*	xow
K2	mee	*	eem	*	*	*	eem

SELECTED BIBLIOGRAPHY

Akrigg, G. P. V. Jacobean Pageant: or The Court of King
     James I. Cambridge, Massachusetts: Harvard
     University Press, 1962.

Anderson, Donald K., Jr. "Kingship in Ford's Perkin
     Warbeck." ELH, 27 (1960), 177-193.

_____. "Richard II and Perkin Warbeck."
     Shakespeare Quarterly, 13 (Spring 1962), 260-263.

_____. "The Heart and the Banquet: Imagery in
     Ford's 'Tis Pity and The Broken Heart." Studies in
     English Literature 1500-1900, 2 (Spring 1962),
     209-17.

_____. John Ford. Twayne English Authors Series.
     New York: Twayne Publishers, 1972.

_____. "John Ford" in The Later Jacobean and
     Caroline Dramatists: A Survey and Bibliography of
     Recent Studies in English Renaissance Drama.
     Lincoln, Nebraska: University of Nebraska Press,
     1978.

Babb, Lawrence. The Elizabethan Malady: A Study of
     Melancholia in English Literature from 1580-1642.
     1951; rpt. East Lansing: Michigan-State University
     Press, 1965.

Bentley, Gerald Eades. The Jacobean and Caroline Stage:
     Plays and Playwrights. 7 vols. Oxford: Claren-
     don Press, 1949-1968.

Blayney, Glenn H. "Convention, Plot and Structure in
     The Broken Heart." Modern Philology, 56 (August
     1958), 1-9.

Brissenden, Alan. "Impediments to Love: A Theme in
     John Ford." Renaissance Drama, 7 (1964), 95-102.

Bueler, Louis E. "Role-Splitting and Reintegration:
     The Tainted Woman Plot in Ford." Studies in
     English Literature, 20 (1980), 325-344.

Burton, Robert. The Anatomy of Melancholy. Eds. Floyd

Dell and Paul Jordan-Smith. 1927; rpt. New York: Tudor Publishing Company, 1938.

Craig, Hardin. The Enchanted Glass: The Elizabethan Mind in Literature. New York: Oxford University Press, 1936.

Danby, John F. Poets on Fortune's Hill: Studies in Sidney, Shakespeare, Beaumont & Fletcher. 1952; rpt. Port Washington, New York: Kennikat Press, Inc., 1966.

Davril, Robert. Le Drame de John Ford. Paris: Bibliotheque des Langues Modernes, 1954.

Eliot, T. S. Selected Essays: 1917-1932. London: Faber and Faber, Limited, 1932.

Ellis, Havelock, ed. John Ford. The Mermaid Series. London: Ernest Benn, Ltd., n.d.

Ellis-Fermor, Una. The Jacobean Drama: An Interpretation. 2nd ed., rev. London: Methuen & Co., Ltd., 1947.

Ewing, S. Blaine. Burtonian Melancholy in the Plays of John Ford. Princeton Studies in English, No. 19. Princeton: Princeton University Press, 1940.

Farr, Dorothy. John Ford and the Caroline Theater. New York: Barnes and Noble, 1978.

Frost, David L. The School of Shakespeare: The Influence of Shakespeare on English Drama, 1600-42. Cambridge: The University Press, 1968.

Harbage, Alfred. Shakespeare and the Rival Traditions. 1952; rpt. New York: Barnes and Noble, Inc., 1968.

_____. Cavalier Drama: An Historical and Critical Supplement to the Study of the Elizabethan and Restoration Stage. 1936; rpt. New York: Russell & Russell, Inc., 1964.

_____. "The Mystery of Perkin Warbeck," Studies in the English Renaissance Drama, eds. Josephine W. Bennett, et al. New York: New York University Press, 1959.

Hawkins, Harriet. "The Morality of Elizabethan Drama: Some Footnotes to Plato" in English Renaissance Studies Presented to Dame Helen Gardner in Honor of her Seventieth Birthday, ed. John Carey. Oxford: Clarendon Press, 1980.

Herrick, Marvin T. Tragicomedy. 1955; rpt. Urbana: University of Illinois Press, 1962.

Howarth, R.G. "John Ford." Notes & Queries, NS 4 (1957), 241.

Hoy, Cyrus. "'Ignorance in Knowledge': Marlowe's Faustus and Ford's Giovanni." Modern Philology, 57 (February 1960), 145-154.

_____. The Hyacinth Room: An Investigation into the Nature of Comedy, Tragedy, & Tragicomedy. New York: Alfred A. Knopf, 1964.

Huebert, Ronald. "'Artificial Way to Grieve': The For- saken Woman Plot in Beaumont and Fletcher, Massinger, and Ford." ELH 44 (1977), 601-621.

_____. John Ford: Baroque English Dramatist. Montreal: McGill-Queen's University Press, 1977.

Kable, William S. "The Influence of Justification on Spelling in Jaggard's Compositor B." Studies in Bibliography, 20 (1967), 235-39.

Kaufman, R. J. "Ford's Tragic Perspective." Texas Studies in Literature and Language, 1 (Winter 1960), 522-537.

Leech, Clifford. John Ford and the Drama of His Time. London: Chatto & Windus, 1957.

Lowell, James Russell. Conversations on Some of the Old Poets. New York: T. Y. Crowell & Co., 1901.

Lynch, Kathleen M. The Social Mode of Restoration Comedy. 1926; rpt. New York: Octagon Books, Inc., 1965.

McDonald, Charles O. "The Design of John Ford's The Broken Heart: A Study in the Development of Caroline Sensibility." Studies in Philology, 59 (1962), 141-161.

McMaster, Juliet. "Love, Lust, and Sham: Structural Pattern in the Plays of John Ford." Renaissance Drama, NS 2 (1969), 157-166.

Morris, Brian, ed. The Broken Heart, by John Ford. The New Mermaids. London: Ernest Benn, Ltd., 1965.

Muir, Kenneth. "The Case for John Ford." Sewanee Review, 84 (1976), 614-629.

Oliver, Harold James. The Problem of John Ford. Carlton, Victoria: Melbourne University Press, 1955.

Orbison, Tucker. The Tragic Vision of John Ford. Jacobean Drama Studies. Salzburg, Austria: Institut für Englische Sprache und Literatur, 1974.

Ornstein, Robert. The Moral Vision of Jacobean Tragedy. Madison: The University of Wisconsin Press, 1960.

Parrott, Thomas Marc and Robert Hamilton Ball. A Short View of Elizabethan Drama. New York: Charles Scribner's Sons, 1943.

Putt, S. Gorley. "The Modernity of John Ford." English, 18 (1969), 47-52.

Reed, Robert Rentoul, Jr. Bedlam on the Jacobean Stage. 1952; rpt. New York: Octagon Books, 1970.

Ribner, Irving. "By Nature's Light: The Morality of 'Tis Pity She's a Whore." Tulane Studies in English, 10 (1960), 39-50.

_____. Jacobean Tragedy: The Quest for Moral Order. New York: Barnes and Noble, Inc., 1962.

Roberts, Jeanne A. "John Ford's Passionate Abstractions," Southern Humanities Review, 7 (1973), 322-332.

Sargeaunt, M. Joan. John Ford. 1935; rpt. New York: Russell & Russell, 1966.

Sensabaugh, George Frank. "John Ford and Elizabethan Tragedy." Philological Quarterly, 20 (July 1941), 442-53.

_____. "John Ford and Platonic Love in the Court."
Studies in Philology, 36 (1939), 206-26

_____. The Tragic Muse of John Ford. Stanford:
Stanford University Press, 1944.

Sherman, Stuart P. "Ford's Contribution to the Decadence of Drama," John Ford's Dramatische Werke.
Ed. W. Bang. Materialien zur Kunde des Alteren
Englischen Dramas. Louvain: Librairie Universitaire, 1908. XXIII, vii-xix.

_____. "Stella and The Broken Heart." PMLA, 24
(1909), 275-85.

Stavig, Mark. John Ford and the Traditional Moral
Order. Madison: The University of Wisconsin
Press, 1968.

Sutton, Juliet. "Platonic Love in Ford's The Fancies,
Chaste and Noble." Studies in English Literature
1500-1900, 7 (Spring 1967), 299-309.

Swinburne, Algernon Charles. "John Ford," The Complete
Works. Eds. Sir Edmund Gosse and Thomas J. Wise.
1925; rpt. New York: Russell & Russell, 1968.
XII, 371-406.

Tannenbaum, Samuel A. John Ford: A Concise Bibliography. Elizabethan Bibliographies, No. 20.
New York: Samuel A. Tannenbaum, 1941.

Tucker, Kenneth. A Bibliography of Writings by and
about John Ford and Cyril Tourneur. Boston:
G. K. Hall and Co., 1977.

Upham, Alfred Horatio. The French Influence in English
Literature: From the Accession of Elizabeth to the
Restoration. 1908; rpt. New York: Octagon Books,
Inc., 1965.

Ure, Peter. "Cult and Initiates in Ford's Love's
Sacrifice." Modern Language Quarterly, 11
(September 1950), 298-306.

Ure, Peter, ed. The Chronicle History of Perkin Warbeck:
A Strange Truth. The Revels Plays. London:
Methuen & Co., Ltd., 1968

Wells, Henry W. Elizabethan and Jacobean Playwrights.
    2nd ed., 1939; rpt. Port Washington, New York:
    Kennikat Press, Inc., 1964.

Wells, Stanley. English Drama (excluding Shakespeare):
    Select Bibliographical Guides. Oxford: Oxford
    University Press, 1975.

For Product Safety Concerns and Information please contact our EU
representative GPSR@taylorandfrancis.com
Taylor & Francis Verlag GmbH, Kaufingerstraße 24, 80331 München, Germany